THE

One-Hat

SOLUTION

Also by the author

Walking the Tightrope
Rogers' Rules for Success

THE
One-Hat
SOLUTION

ROGERS' STRATEGY
FOR
CREATIVE MIDDLE
MANAGEMENT

Henry C. Rogers

St. Martin's Press
NEW YORK

A *Disclaimer*

This book was written for both men and women; every anecdote, every illustration, every "rule" in this book is equally applicable to either sex. I had originally tried, therefore, to use a mixture of the pronouns *he* and *she*. When I found myself writing "When he or she goes to his or her office," however, I knew I was in trouble. I have given in to the demands of the language, and the following text features the masculine pronoun. Please be assured that this is in no way meant to exclude female readers.

Design by Stanley S. Drate/Folio Graphics Co., Inc.

Library of Congress Cataloging in Publication Data

Rogers, Henry C., 1914-
   The one-hat solution.

   1. Success in business.   2. Psychology, Industrial.
I. Title.
HF5386.R5444   1986   650.1   86-13841
ISBN 0-312-58524-1

First Edition

10 9 8 7 6 5 4 3 2 1

To Roz, Marcia, Ron, Melissa and Michael, the most important people in my life, to my partner Warren, and to my associates and clients, past and present, who have given me the material on which this book is based.

Contents

Introduction

There are millions of you out there. You work in high-rise office buildings in New York, Chicago, Los Angeles, Philadelphia, Boston, Atlanta, and fifty other major metropolitan centers throughout the country. You also work in smaller cities and towns from Spokane to Escondido in the West, from Bangor to Key West in the East, from Missoula to Baton Rouge in the great Midwest. You work in industrial plants, on farms and ranches, in banks, real estate offices, insurance companies, high-tech firms, hotels, and hospitals.

Who are you? Though you are husbands, wives, sons and daughters, widows and widowers, in your twenties and in your sixties, you all fit into one category of our nation's economy. You are *middle management*.

> *You are an employee; you report to a boss.*
> *You are also a boss; employees report to you.*

You are two people in one body. You have one brain but two areas of responsibility. You wear a "boss" hat with your subordinates and an "employee" hat with your boss. You are an actor playing two roles on the same stage in the same play—simultaneously.

Not surprisingly, at times many of you feel like budding schizophrenics. Middle management can be stressful: you may find the constant transition from boss to employee and back to boss a challenging and often frustrating experience. Although you know when to put your boss hat on and when to take it off, your problem is that the recurrent changing of hats can result in confusion, inconsistency, equivocation, and tension, both for yourself and for those above and below you on the office totem pole. I call this syndrome *the two-hat problem.*

I have long been a student of the behavior of middle management people in my own organization. Many of them are chameleons. When, as employees, they meet with me or my partner Warren Cowan, they are one person. Ten minutes later when they meet with the employees who report to them, they become entirely different people. They are Dr. Jekyll one moment, Mr. Hyde the next.

From where I sit, this is not merely your problem, it's *my* problem, or rather, *our* problem. All this flip-flopping back and forth is not only bad for you, it's bad for productivity. To deal with this two-hat problem, I have developed what I call the *one-hat solution.* As a middle manager, it will save a lot of wear and tear on your emotional state if you can be the same person when you discuss a problem with your boss that you are when you're dealing with your own staff. Are you a bit servile with your boss and a bit overbearing with your subordinates? You'll find that your world will run more smoothly if you treat them both alike—with respect, dignity, and sensitivity.

The best bosses and the best staff members I know conduct

themselves by the same rules of behavior: they're nice to people, don't put them down, make them feel important, put them at ease. It may sound corny, but the best and most basic Rogers' Rule is the Golden Rule: Do Unto Others as You Would Have Them Do Unto You. Treat your employees as you would like your boss to treat you. Talk with them as you would like him to talk with you. Conduct a meeting with them as you would like your boss to conduct his meetings. If you have the perfect boss, your job is easy. If he leaves much to be desired, just imagine how you would like him to be—and act accordingly with your subordinates.

Take a look at yourself. First, from your boss's perspective. Imagine yourself behind his desk. Imagine yourself in his shoes. Imagine yourself as your boss would see you. Are you the same person you saw when you looked at yourself in the mirror this morning?

If you think you are, I suggest that you take a deeper, more incisive, more objective look. We rarely realize or admit our own inadequacies and our own faults. If we do, we have a tendency to rationalize and make excuses for them. Be honest with yourself. Make a list titled "How my boss now perceives me."

Now look again. Imagine that the people who report to you are at this very moment having a bull session. Try to imagine what they're saying.

I know how tough it is. I got a taste of it one day. I used to think that I was the perfect boss until one day Warren Cowan and I got into a discussion about one of our employees. Warren suggested that I should try harder to establish a better relationship with Roy, one of our middle management associates.

"It's strange," I said. "I never seem to talk with Roy. He never comes to see me. In fact, I never even see him. Where does he hide?"

Warren laughed. "Don't you know why you never see him?"

"I have no idea," was my reply.

"He's afraid of you. He's in awe of you. He makes a point of avoiding you. When he sees you approaching, he runs the other way."

"Oh, come on," I said. "I don't believe you. Why would anyone be afraid of me? Awe? Why would anyone be in awe of me?"

Warren shook his head back and forth, laughed again, and said, "You just don't know the impression you make on a lot of people around here. They're scared to death of you."

I was really disturbed. I genuinely thought I was easily approachable, affable, easy to talk to, smiling, friendly, benevolent. The idea that any one of our employees would be frightened of me was just inconceivable.

I couldn't accept what Warren had said, so I suggested that right then on the spot we confront a few of our senior management people. Warren agreed. A few moments later we were all gathered in my office.

"You guys have to level with me," I said. "Warren just told me that Roy and a lot of other people around here are afraid of me and run the other way when they see me coming. I don't believe him. Is it true?"

The three of them looked at each other, looked at Warren, looked at me.

Warren encouraged them. "Go ahead, tell him. He's asking you to level with him."

They all confirmed what Warren had said. I shook my head in wonderment. I had had no idea. I thanked them for their candor, and after they had gone I thanked Warren too for having pointed out my own inadequacies in my relationships with our employees. Once I discovered the truth, I started to make an attempt to change the impression that middle management people had of me. Although I am sure that I haven't solved the problem entirely, I know that I have improved.

I point this out to tell you that it is unlikely you really know what your boss and your employees think of you, and that it is time you found out.

Now you are to make a second list. You can title it "How I am perceived by the people who report to me."

This second list will come easier to you than the first one did. You are now becoming aware that you are not the person you thought you were—but rather the person who others think you are. You are beginning to see yourself from a different perspective. It happened to me. I am sure it will happen to you, too.

Where do you go from here? The time has come to make some changes in your work style. It is time to devise a new set of rules for yourself—rules that will help you to improve your performance both as an employer and as an employee. You are the captain of your own team and you are also a player on your boss's team. The skills you require to get the best possible performance from your subordinates are exactly the same skills you need to *inspire* your boss to *motivate* you.

What gives me the right to pontificate in this fashion? Who am I that I am qualified to give you advice? I'm Henry Rogers, chairman—executive committee of Rogers & Cowan, one of the largest public relations firms in the country, with over two hundred employees and a client list that includes distinguished companies and personalities in the world of entertainment as well as numerous Fortune 500 corporations.

I am writing this book based on my own personal experiences. Although I never had a boss as such (I started my own one-man publicity business at the age of twenty-one), I have always had many bosses. Every client was and is a boss. Thus, I can relate to you not only as the founder of a successful public relations firm, but as the "employee" of many hundreds of clients over a period of many, many years.

There was a time in my career when I became dissatisfied with my own performance in the public relations business. I felt that my relationships with my clients didn't satisfy the standards I had set for myself and that my skills in the area of employee relations were not at the level they should be if I intended to be truly successful. I began to study other people, entrepreneurs and executives with companies large and small. I studied the successful people I knew and tried to find one key factor that served as a common denominator for all of them. I discounted the obvious traits that all successful people have. I ignored self-esteem, will, hard work, energy, drive, talent, and self-control. I knew that you need those qualifications and many more in varying degrees to be successful, but I was looking for something more obscure, something deeper, intellectual. Then one day it came to me. I went back and looked at all the same people again. Yes, it was true. Yes, all of them had the knack of being able to *sell themselves* to other people. They were skilled in *people relations*. I didn't know whether this quality was genetic or acquired, or whether they practiced it consciously or unconsciously. I did realize that people relations had as much—or perhaps even more—to do with their success than any of their other professional skills.

I discovered that the ability to relate to people is an invaluable asset. It gives those who are striving for success a leg up on those who are unaware of the rewards that come to those who hone their people relations skills. That discovery changed my life, and my career began to move ahead more rapidly.

I started with the premise that I had to learn to sell myself to other people. I gradually became aware that the use of psychology was becoming a factor in the development of my relationships with both my clients and my associates. Then one day I coined a word that described the program of thinking and behavior that I had been developing: *psychorelations*. I now consider psychorelations to be a critical skill. It is critical because it determines the quality of one's relationship with people, which in turn determines one's level of success. Psychorelations is the tool we use to sell ourselves to other people. Psychorelations is people relations elevated to the highest level. It became the theme of my most recent book, *Rogers' Rules for Success*.

Now I return to you, the reader. What does all this have to do with you? You are going to use the principles of psychorelations to better manage your boss and motivate your employees and to help yourself "wear one hat." You have your lists in front of you, lists indicating how you believe your boss perceives you and how your employees perceive you. Now make two more lists:

1. How I would *like* my boss to perceive me
2. How I would *like* my employees to perceive me

Look at all four lists. First look at yourself as an employee. I'm sure you can see a big difference between the two lists. Now look at yourself as an employer. Again, there is a big difference.

What do you want? You want to get those lists to be as nearly identical as possible. You want your employer and your employees to perceive you as you would like them to perceive you.

You will accomplish your objective by first learning the basic principles of psychorelations. You will learn to sell yourself to your employer—and by doing so *manage* him. You will learn to sell yourself to your employees and by doing so *motivate* them. All of this becomes possible, probable, and *doable*, if you remember that your *two-hat problem has a one-hat solution*.

The one-hat solution takes the psychorelations technique one step further and applies it specifically to middle management. Do you want to learn how to motivate your employees? There's more to it than telling them what to do—a lot more. In the coming chapters you will learn how to give instructions and delegate responsibility, how to make your subordinates *want* to do more and do better. You will learn that you can motivate your boss in much the same way.

Motivate a boss? It's not a contradiction in terms. In fact, it's one of the best things you can do for yourself on the way up. You will learn how to deal with troublesome and troubled office personalities—whether they are employees or (much touchier) your boss. A touchy boss requires kid gloves. I'll show you how to approach him and his ego so that you can get along with him and enjoy a productive working relationship with a difficult individual.

How can you do this without turning into a yes-man? Rogers has rules on the art of saying no gracefully. The principles in *The One-Hat Solution* helped bring me to the top of my field. When I've made mistakes, I've almost always been able to trace them back to a violation of one of my own rules. But making mistakes is okay (you'll learn about that, too), so I will tell you about some of mine and what I've learned from them.

The One-Hat Solution represents not only the best of my thinking, but the input of other successful executives as well. While preparing this book, I contacted many top-level bosses, asking how they dealt with some of the major issues covered in these chapters. The response was both valuable and validating. Although each executive has his own personal style, their answers confirmed my faith in my own principles and the one-hat solution. The constructive use of humor and diplomacy, the value of helping subordinates grow in their jobs, dishing out praise at proper times, and most of all the importance of letting those above you and below you on the management ladder know you care about them as human beings—these are common threads that run through all the responses I received. Throughout this book you will find not only "Rogers' Rules," but anecdotes and suggestions from top-level executives in all fields of business. I believe you will find the information in the chapters that follow useful guidelines for successful middle management and a path to follow that will help you to boost yourself up one day into the big-boss ranks.

1

Help Is a Two-Way Street

There are employers and employees because one person can't do everything by him- or herself. You can't do what your boss does, do what your subordinates do, and handle your own job all at the same time. That is why, unless you one day become a chief executive officer, you will always report to someone who is a slot above you on the organization chart, and you will have people reporting to you. Come to think of it, even if you one day become a C.E.O., you will still be accountable to a board of directors.

The assignment of tasks—from you to your subordinates or from your boss to you—is the basis of all your interoffice relationships. It should be the easiest part of your job, but the process, for numerous complex reasons, is fraught with pitfalls, misunderstandings, and stress.

The ideal relationship between you and your employees is symbiotic: you and your employees will both be happier when they are performing well. They were hired to help you, but to do so, they need to know specifically what they are supposed to do. Why, if it is as simple as it sounds, do so many managers find themselves in trouble, with staffs who are not doing what they are asked to do? These managers, and you may be among them, eventually discover that the reason the job is not getting done is that the staff has been receiving unclear directions. No one has spelled out specifically what is expected of them, or even when it is expected.

You wonder why they don't speak up and say, "What is it that you're asking me to do? What do I do first?" Why don't they? For the very same reason that you have been giving them fuzzy directives: *fear.*

You hate the thought. You're certain that it doesn't apply to you. But let's think about it for a while. You're not entirely satisfied with the performance of your subordinates. The reason may well be a lack of specific direction from you. Maybe you haven't told them what you thought you told them. Maybe that's the reason they do the little things, not the big things.

Why haven't you been clear? It could stem from fear. You may have a fear of letting go. You don't trust them to handle the important assignments, because you're certain that you can handle them better yourself. Of course you can. That's why you were elevated to the middle management ranks, but now your first responsibility is to *motivate others to do what you had been doing.* You will not be a successful manager *until you learn to let go.*

Now think about your own relationship with your boss. Are you faced with a similar situation with him? Do you feel that he should turn over more responsibility to you? Do you believe that he should hand you some of those important assignments that he keeps for himself? Why doesn't he? We are probably dealing with the same situation: fear. He probably believes you can't do it as well as he can. He fears letting go. He doesn't completely trust your abilities. You and your boss are much alike. What to do about it? How do you solve the problem of being comfortable with turning over greater authority to your subordinates and convincing your boss to turn over some of his responsibilities to you?

Overcoming Fear and Building Trust

The way to fight fear in the office is with trust. Once an understanding has been built between you and your subordinates and between you and your boss, everything else you have to do will become much easier. But how do you build trust to the point that you and your boss can both overcome your fears about letting go? The answer is to get to know your people better, develop a relationship with them, develop a closer understanding with them. How do you develop this symbiotic understanding? You are dealing with a fragile relationship, and a high-maintenance one at that. You, your boss, and your subordinates spend more time together during a day than most husbands and wives do. You must live together, work together, relate to each other.

The amount of "togetherness" you have in your office is a matter of individual executive style. Mark McCormack, author of the bestseller *What They Don't Teach You at Harvard Business School*, says he doesn't socialize with his employees after office hours. In contrast, Richard Kress, president of Norelco, told me he won't hire anyone unless he feels comfortable inviting them to his home to play poker. Two contrasting styles; they both work. The one essential factor, however, is a high level of understanding during office hours.

This brings us back to psychorelations. As I wrote earlier, it is the tool we use to sell ourselves to other people. Office understanding is built by the continual process of simultaneously selling yourself to your boss and selling yourself to those who report to you. And you do this by finding out what those above you and below you care about, by putting yourself in the other person's shoes.

Selling yourself must be done one on one. Staff meetings are not the answer because each person's needs, ambitions, and motivations are different. It probably means a series of individual meetings, often casual and unscheduled—a coffee break, a drink at the local bar after hours, a chat in the car on the way to a meeting. You will find the key to each person through gentle probing and digging. People are often reluctant to say outright what they want, what they aspire to. You will discover that a word dropped here and there will give you a clue, a key to what motivates each of them. Some want to be team captain; others just want to be part of the loyal support troops. Some want to be praised, others want "tender loving care." Some need their self-image bolstered, some are motivated only by money, and others care only about security and a sense of belonging. And there are always those who don't know what they want.

This is not the time to be a police detective in the interrogation room. Think of yourself more like Angela Lansbury as Jessica Fletcher in "Murder, She Wrote" or Peter Falk with his rumpled raincoat in the old "Columbo" series. Making small talk in the office is not wasting time. People reveal themselves in unguarded moments, not when they're on the defensive.

Finally, if you work at it, you will develop trust; you will overcome fear; you will finally begin to let go. You will begin to give your subordinates specific instructions. You will arrive at a point where you and they will have a complete understanding about priorities. You will all be working on the same wavelength—and while that is happening, don't be surprised if you discover that trust works both ways. Once you begin to trust the troops, you will find that your boss will begin to place his trust in you. The explanation for this anomaly is not a difficult one. As you become a more trusting person, you begin to exude confidence. You take on an air of self-assurance and self-esteem that was not apparent before. With this new "you" in the spotlight, your boss's fear of turning over some of his responsibilities to you will gradually disappear; he will come to realize that your newly acquired trust and confidence in those around you has made you a better manager. You trust them—he will trust you.

You can help this process by pursuing a closer relationship with him. Encourage his trust in you by telling him about the success you are having with your subordinates. He will quickly understand what you're trying to tell him: "It's working for me; it will work for you too." Don't hang back. Don't be afraid. Find opportunities to meet with him. Don't wait for him to ask for a meeting. Jump the gun. Ask him before he asks you. Don't be concerned about being rejected once or twice. The first time you suggest having coffee with him before the office opens in the morning or a drink after five or six o'clock, he may turn you down. Try again. Your boss may be one of the exceptions who will not respond to your encouraging a closer relationship with him. Then it's time to back away. But at least you tried and he's not going to resent you for trying. Your next boss may be more receptive.

ROGERS' RULES FOR OVERCOMING FEAR AND BUILDING TRUST

1. **Be tolerant.** If you're going to find out what people are like, you have to accept them the way they are, not the way you would

like them to be. Try to understand who they are on their own terms, without judging them.

2. **Never underestimate the Power of Lunch.** You can probably find out more about people during a meal than at any other time. Don't make your luncheon invitation an abrupt, out-of-context act. Build your relationship first. Then, at an opportune moment, say, "Let's have lunch."

3. **Look for habit patterns, preferences.** Is your new employee a dyed-in-the-wool yuppie or a down-home kid from the country? A family man or a confirmed bachelor? Is your boss patient and reasonable after lunch but a bear first thing Monday morning? Put the pieces together.

4. **Never betray a confidence.** Trust and understanding go hand in hand.

5. **Don't be so busy probing to understand other people that you clam up yourself.** Let them get to know and understand you.

Passing the Baton

To be an effective manager, you must motivate your people by trusting them to make their own decisions within the framework you have established for them. You expect that from your boss. Your employees expect it and should receive it from you.

You may find it very difficult to delegate authority because you feel that it detracts from your own capabilities, or at least from your own sense of importance. How false that assumption is and how shallow this thinking is! A good manager is one who can motivate his people to take on authority and responsibility so that the boss is free to think about the "big picture"—how his department can get better and more profitable, how it can produce a greater contribution to the company.

Give that some thought. If you are able to turn responsibility over to others, it makes you more, not less, important. As for your role as an employee, remember that a good employee is one who gives his boss the gift of time and a sense of assurance that the assignments he turns over to you have been placed in capable hands.

"In capable hands"—that is the key—both for you and your employees. Your boss wants you to make decisions, and you want your subordinates to make decisions. What decisions? How much authority do you want them to have? Before you make your own decision on this vital subject, study your department first. If you have just inherited a department that has been working efficiently under your predecessor, my advice is to not rock the boat. Don't screw around with success—at least not until you have had time to study the operation to determine whether there are areas that can be improved. If your predecessor gave his associates full authority, let them keep it. If he gave them little authority, then start turning responsibilities over to them slowly but deliberately. Don't do anything abruptly or you may well have chaos on your hands.

If in contrast you have inherited an ineffectively run operation, don't try to be a hero overnight. Talk to your new subordinates. Get input from them and then begin to restructure, turning responsibilities over to them step by step, watching every new development as it progresses. Your goal, of course, is to turn decision-making over to your subordinates, but make certain before you do that they are capable of making those decisions and are ready to make them.

The advantages of delegating responsibility and authority to others was brought home to me for the first time shortly after Rogers & Cowan was established in 1950. During the years before then when I'd been in business by myself, I would never have thought of taking a vacation. Warren Cowan worked on me for a long time before he finally convinced me, in 1952, that the business wouldn't fall apart if I took a vacation. My wife Roz and I started planning and left for our first trip to Europe in June. We were gone for five weeks; the trip still remains in my mind as the best holiday I ever had. The first week, however, was hell (probably not just for me, but for Roz and Warren as well). I called the office daily to find out whether the business was still there. I was like a junkie addicted to my business responsibilities, eight thousand miles from the office and suffering from acute withdrawal. Finally Warren, doubtless at his wits' end, scolded me and told me that he was going to refuse to answer the telephone the next time I called.

Five weeks later I returned, shocked to find that no one had missed me. No clients had discharged Rogers & Cowan because Henry wasn't there. None of our employees were disturbed or insecure because I hadn't been there. In fact, much to my chagrin and delight, business had actually improved. It was the first time it became apparent that no one is indispensable—not even me.

The key to this successful vacation was that it forced me to trust my partner to run the business in my absence. The fact is that I didn't completely trust him until he screamed at me on the telephone one day, "Get off my back." Then I had no choice. I realized that if I didn't "let go" immediately, I would be chained to my desk fifty-two weeks a year for the rest of my life. I've gotten better at delegating authority since then, but I still have occasional lapses.

Dick Taylor joined our firm a number of years ago. He proved himself particularly adept; his skills multiplied and he eventually became president of our corporate division. We gave him full authority to operate with that title, and he took on awesome responsibilities.

When Mattel, Inc., asked us to make a public relations presentation to handle Barbie Doll, however, Dick was away. I made the presentation in his absence and we were awarded the contract. Dick returned a few days later but, inexplicably, I didn't let go. I didn't let him assume responsibility for a project that should by long-standing company policy have been under his jurisdiction. It was exactly the kind of assignment that he had proved himself eminently capable of handling in the past, but my ego evidently got in the way. Either that or I must have fallen in love with Barbie. There seems to be no other explanation.

It was almost a disaster. As we neared the end of our first year, we had an unhappy, dissatisfied client. I was trying to be the account supervisor and serve as chairman of our company at the same time. It didn't work. I finally saw the light and put Dick back in charge, where he should have been all along. Luckily Mattel was willing to give us a chance to make amends and do it right—the way Dick would have done it from the beginning if I'd only had the sense to let go.

Gordon Stulberg, president of Polygram Corporation, told me that he once took a big gamble in an important business negotiation because he decided to delegate authority in this matter to one of his associates.

"I entrusted the disposition of a division of one of the corporations that I managed," he said, "to a senior executive who was very anxious to prove himself in this area. After a series of meetings with an interested buyer, it became apparent that he was intent on "winning" and as a result, the negotiations were mired in a series of disputes about points that he had made as matters of "principle." Rather than simply suggesting that he concede the points, I reviewed the negotiations with him carefully and asked him what he considered to be the three principal items vital to closing the deal. He clearly recognized and shared my feelings about what the principal elements were that had to be achieved. I then left it entirely up to his judgment as to how to handle these and other points that he had become enmeshed with. I knew that having identified the principal areas in this way, his own common sense and judgment would lead him to either compromise or withdraw from lesser points that he had made an issue about. Had I, on the other hand, dictated what I thought were the principal areas and what should be done about what I personally considered minor issues, it would have been a severe disservice to our relationship. Ultimately, of course, he closed the deal and his loyalty was secure, even though by taking that course of action, I had to take the chance that his ego involvement with the minor issues might have killed the entire negotiation."

This was a case of an executive who turned over responsibility to an associate, but remained available for counsel and advice when it was needed.

ROGERS' RULES FOR DELEGATING AUTHORITY

1. List the tasks you perform regularly as part of your job. Which of those duties could you delegate to someone under you?

2. In general, let the person closest to a problem handle as much of it as he can. Don't step in at the last minute to make the big decisions just because you're the boss.

3. When you delegate, let go. Don't hover. You don't need a blow-by-blow description to be kept informed. Have your subordinates report to you on results, not details.

4. Have human-sized, not superhuman, expectations. No one can do your job as well as you can, but one or more of your subordinates can almost certainly do it well enough. Your unreasonable expectations can make others afraid to take on

added responsibilities that could adversely affect their job performance.

5. List the tasks your boss performs. Which of these jobs do you feel qualified to take on?

6. Make it easy for your boss to delegate tasks to you. Do you know which part of his job your boss absolutely hates? See if he's willing to delegate all or part of that responsibility to you.

7. Volunteer to lend a hand to your boss, but approach it gingerly. You're trying to help someone without giving the impression that you're out to steal his job. Say, "Next time you're working on _____, I'd like to pitch in and lend a hand. It's something I'm interested in and I know that it takes up a lot of your time."

Establishing Priorities

Whether you delegate tasks to subordinates or take them on from those above you, it is essential that it be clear precisely what the assignment is and where it fits in the overall scheme of things. When in doubt, ask. For many years I had the same problem that many business executives face—determining priorities for myself. I finally solved that problem by establishing on a month-by-month, week-by-week, day-by-day basis, what is truly important and what can be relegated to second position. At times, however, I still run into trouble with a tendency to fail to come to an understanding with my associates as to what their priorities should be.

George walked into my office one day, slouched onto my couch and announced, "We have to talk."

"Sure," I said. "Any time."

"Right now," he said, slumping lower into the furniture. I was getting the impression that something was amiss.

"What's the matter?" I asked. "Something wrong?"

"You're damned right something's wrong," he barked. "I've been up all night trying to figure out this problem. I've decided there's no solution. I shouldn't be working here any longer. I used to like my job, but for two cents I'd quit and look elsewhere, if I had the guts."

I was dumbfounded. George was one of our best supervisors. He related well to clients; he was professional; he got along well with his peers. Not only that, I liked him very much personally and thought he had a glowing future with our organization. "So what's the problem?" I asked naively.

"You!" he replied. "You're what's wrong."

It wasn't tactful, but he certainly got my attention. I was astonished. "Me? You must be kidding!" I said, completely perplexed at this turn of events.

"Yes, you! You're driving me crazy and I just can't handle it anymore. I'm at the end of my rope."

I swallowed my surprise long enough to say, "Okay, let's talk this one out. If I'm driving you crazy I'm really sorry, but I don't realize it. Tell me what I'm doing that disturbs you so much."

He looked at me again. Was there a hint of anger, even hatred, in his eyes? I was shattered. I thought he liked me and that we understood each other. "You're on my back all the time. I work my buns off around here. I put in ten and twelve hours a day, and when you walk in here on a Saturday or Sunday afternoon you still find me here, pounding on a typewriter or catching up on the reports and memos I hadn't gotten to all week. No one puts in the kind of time I do, no one cares about his job or the company the way I do, and you're still on my back."

As angry as he was, I was fortunate that he was still willing to talk it over. It took awhile, but when we finally discovered the source of the problem, we were both surprised to see how simple it was, how basic. There was no denying the number of hours George put in; there was also no denying that I'd been tough on him lately. The problem was *priorities*. We were poles apart. He was busting his butt on stuff I didn't think was important while neglecting matters that were uppermost in my mind.

The fault was entirely mine. I had never explained in sufficient detail what I thought George's priorities should be. He had no idea what I believed to be important—what should be done immediately, what could be done tomorrow or next week or next month—or what didn't have to be done at all. I had left him guessing, more or less inventing his own job. No wonder George was frustrated; inadvertently, I'd been criticizing him for not doing what he didn't know I expected him to do. We've long since patched up our differences, but I learned an important lesson from George. I now work more closely with all my associates and come to agreements with them on their priorities. I usually do not assign priorities. Instead, we arrive at them through discussion and compromise, which results in total understanding and agreement.

There was further benefit to my meeting with George. Upon reflection I realized that the problem I had with George was similar to one we occasionally have with a dissatisfied client. We feel that we are doing a terrific job, but the client keeps voicing complaints. We then realize that we are eating from different plates. We are concentrating on oranges, not realizing that the client's primary concern is apples. Once we come to an agreement with the client on priorities, the problems disappear.

When Diahann Carroll was first assigned to a role in "Dynasty," she became a client of Rogers & Cowan. This was her first television series since "Julia" many years before. For career reasons, she hoped to receive as much media coverage as John Forsythe, Linda Evans, and Joan Collins did. This coverage, she felt, would give her added leverage in getting a juicy role in another television series if and when "Dynasty" ever closed down production.

I was surprised when our account executive who was assigned to represent Ms. Carroll told me one day that she would like to meet with me sometime at our mutual convenience. This came as a surprise because I had phased out of representing personality clients many years before. That end of our business had long been supervised by Warren Cowan and handled by numerous talented vice-presidents and account executives in our public relations agency.

"What does she want to see me about?" I asked.

"I have no idea," came the reply, "but she asked that you set up a date with her secretary because she's working at the studio all day every day."

I didn't mind. I have always been a great admirer of Diahann Carroll, and I regarded the opportunity to have a meeting with such a beautiful woman as a privilege rather than an obligation. We finally agreed to meet at my home on Saturday at four. In order to be prepared for the meeting I met with Brad, our account executive, who gave me a complete briefing on what we had been doing for her. It sounded good to me. Diahann Carroll must be very pleased with our efforts, I thought, but then what does she want to meet with me about?

Saturday at four, Ms. Carroll arrived at my home, resplendent in a white gabardine pants suit. She was followed a few minutes later by her manager, Roy Gerber, a longtime friend and business acquaintance of mine.

We chatted, I served diet drinks all around, and then it was time for business.

"I'm curious," I said, "as to why you wanted to meet with me. I'm delighted and flattered, but I'm still curious."

She flashed her best, most dazzling Diahann Carroll smile at me and replied, "First, I want to tell you how pleased I am at the way I'm being represented by Rogers & Cowan. Brad, George, and Jeffrey have been devoted as well as creative, and I couldn't be happier, but I'm here because I need some advice. When I was told that you were the founder of the firm, I knew that you were the man I wanted to see."

"Again, I'm flattered," I said. "Tell me your problem."

"I told you that I'm happy with Rogers & Cowan but I'm still not getting what I want," she started.

That sounded paradoxical to me. "How can you be happy if you're not getting what you want?" I asked.

"Because your associates are knocking themselves out getting me an enormous amount of publicity coverage, but I really don't care about any of it. I'm only interested in getting on magazine covers. I feel that at this point in my career, it's the only thing that's important."

"Do you know why you're not getting on magazine covers?" I asked.

"Of course I do," she replied. "Brad and George have talked to every magazine editor in the country. They all say the same thing. Diahann Carroll can't help them sell magazines on the newsstand. That's why I came to you. I thought you might come up with an idea that would get those editors to change their minds."

We talked for twenty minutes about the personalities who appeared on the covers of *People*, *Life*, *Us*, *Ladies Home Journal*, *McCalls*, and other publications that use movie and television personalities on their covers. Diahann already knew the answer to her problem, but I kept stressing that editors kept their jobs by selling magazines, and they were convinced that Diahann's likeness on their covers would not increase their newsstand sales.

"How can you convince them otherwise?" asked the un-daunted, persistent Diahann. I suddenly had an idea. I turned to Roy.

"Roy, do you know what effect, if any, Diahann's first appear-ance on 'Dynasty' had on the Neilsen ratings? Did they stay the same, did they go down, or did they go up?"

"I don't know, but I can find out," he replied.

"I think that might be the answer," I said to Diahann. "If the Neilsen ratings went up in even a half-dozen major cities the week you made your first appearance on 'Dynasty,' that could be the convincing argument we need. A higher rating that night could have signified that a couple of million people tuned in to 'Dynasty' just to see you. We could make a case that these same people will buy a magazine because you are on the cover, in addition to the readers who normally buy the magazine on the newsstand."

Diahann smiled. "I knew I was right in coming to see you. That may be the answer. Let's hope the ratings say what we want them to." She stood up, kissed me on the cheek, and said, "Thanks for seeing me—and on a Saturday too."

I walked her to the front door, and as she left, she made a parting comment, which is the whole point of this story. "Tell George and Brad," she said, "that I appreciate all they've done for me, but they should forget everything else and concentrate on the magazine covers. That's my priority."

Later I discovered that we had been spending some twenty percent of our Diahann Carroll time on covers, but eighty percent on other media outlets. We changed our priorities to suit the client's wishes. Fortunately, my guess was correct. The ratings on "Dynasty" had increased the first night she appeared on the show. That, plus the increased time spent on our client's number-one priority, resulted in her appearance on a number of magazine covers in the months that followed our meeting.

Inasmuch as my client corresponds to your boss, I can now tell you that one of the most important factors in learning how to "handle" your boss is to come to an understanding with him as to what your priorities should be. Here, too, you must remember that you're not wearing two hats. Determining priorities with your boss is just as important as establishing priorities for your subordinates. Before going any further, you should understand the *he* or *she* is your number-one priority.

Do you understand what your relationship to your boss really is? Read this carefully. Get it straight. He is your client. He is your customer. He is the one you must satisfy, please, and impress. You will build your career by performing at peak level, of course, but you and your boss must agree on what peak level is. What do you have to accomplish in order to warrant a pay increase? What is expected of you in order for you to move up the corporate ladder? What is the yardstick? What are the guidelines? What are the priorities?

ROGERS' RULES FOR PRIORITIES

1. Make certain that you and your boss are in accord on your priorities. Make certain that you and your subordinates are in accord on theirs.

2. Ask your boss to give you a list of what he considers to be your priorities. Then prepare your own list. Discuss the two lists with him and arrive at an understanding. Then put the agreed-upon list in writing. Two copies: one for him, one for you. No chance for misunderstanding; it's all there on paper.

3. Follow the same procedure with your subordinates. You have a copy; each of them has a copy. Once more, no chance for misunderstanding. They know what you expect of them, and what they expect of themselves.

4. Don't let the priority lists get lost in the files. Review them regularly with your boss, and your subordinates. How are you doing? How are they doing? You will find that these priority lists will be your best measuring device for performance.

Feedback and Coaching

Brief encounter at the water cooler:

"I heard poor Ralph is gonna get the axe today."

"Yeah, poor guy. He has no idea it's coming, either."

There are any number of violations of Rogers' Rules in this little melodrama, which is repeated far too often in offices across America. If I overheard this conversation in our offices, I would go straight to Ralph's immediate superior and (assuming the rumor was true) raise bloody murder.

Leaving aside the fact that Ralph should be the first, not the last, to know he's being fired, his case would be serious evidence that the feedback and coaching mechanism has entirely broken down. The symbiotic relationship we are trying to maintain between bosses and employees cannot exist unless people know when they're doing a good job—and also when they're doing poorly. No one should ever be totally surprised when he is fired. As a manager, you should be giving your subordinates feedback about their performances, helping them to do better, letting them know—nicely—where they need improvement.

Howard P. Allen, chairman of the board and chief executive officer of the Southern California Edison Company, says it in a nutshell: "I have found the best way is not to try to be cute or textbookish, but merely to be frank and honest, with a few grains of human understanding. Most humans want to do right and do well. Many of them just don't understand what is expected of them. They will work harder and better if they are informed in an understanding and sensitive, but fair and straightforward way. Working with a large organization is merely a multiple of working with individuals, and it all gets down to treating others the way you would like to be treated, realizing that each of us has human deficiencies and all of us would like to do better."

Donald E. Petersen, chairman and chief executive officer of Ford Motor Company, told me, "Feedback and coaching for employees is best accomplished as an ongoing dialogue, not in occasional reviews. Praise and support good performance," he says, "and make suggestions that are constructive."

In addition to giving your subordinates feedback and coaching, you must encourage your boss to give *you* feedback and coaching. You have seen how helpful you can be to your subordinates. Sublimate your ego and understand that your boss probably has knowledge and insights that you don't. Don't be reluctant to pump information out of him. If you can get him to become your mentor, that will help you immensely. If he is not ready for that kind of responsibility, you can still pick his brain.

I went to see a friend of mine one day to ask him for advice. He knew something that I didn't, and I wanted to have as much information on the subject as he did. When we finished our conversation, I was about to leave, when suddenly he said, "Wait a minute, I just thought of something that I want to talk with you about." I sat down.

"We've been sitting here for half an hour. You've been asking me questions, and I've been answering them. It just dawned on me. You're a brain picker." He laughed. I didn't know for a moment whether he had complimented or insulted me. I thought about it for a moment. I had never considered my style of seeking information, of asking questions, in connection with that specific term before. A brain picker? I loved it. I would regard it as a compliment.

"You're right," I replied. "I am a brain picker. I guess I always have been. I just never thought about it before. You see," I explained, "I believe that most people are genuinely good and giving. They want to be helpful. They want to impart their knowledge to other people, but they rarely do it, because no one ever asks them. Most of us are reluctant to ask for advice, ashamed or embarrassed about picking someone's brain. I'm not. I do it all the time. Whenever I have a problem and don't know how to solve it, I look around for someone who I consider to be an expert in the field. Fortunately I have a broad range of contacts and I can always find someone to help me. I'm curious as to why more people aren't brain pickers."

My friend nodded. "You're right," he said. "You've convinced me. I'm going to be a brain picker too. I have some questions about public relations. Can I pick your brain?"

"You certainly can," I replied. We made a lunch date for the following week, and I answered all of his many questions about our business.

You should be a brain picker with your boss. He knows a great deal about many things that you should know. You must overcome your reluctance to pursue him. He may just be waiting for you to ask. Find out how he manages his boss. How did he arrive at his present position? How has he been able to keep his secretary so long? Does he read certain books to sharpen his skills? What does he really get out of those seminars he goes to? Keep asking him questions. Some bosses give feedback and coaching naturally. Others don't. If your boss doesn't, you can achieve the same effect for yourself by being a brain picker.

ROGERS' RULES ON FEEDBACK AND COACHING

1. Don't be the weak link in the chain. Make yourself available to evaluate work completed by your subordinates. Make sure your boss knows what you're up to.

2. Don't gum up the works. If you want to see something in its "final form" before it goes out, give people enough time to make the last-minute changes you suggest.

3. Don't wait until you are seriously unhappy with someone's performance before letting him know. By the time you get around to telling him, the situation may no longer be retrievable.

4. If you suspect your boss is displeased with you but reluctant to say anything, ask for a meeting to discuss it. It may be uncomfortable for you, but you stand an excellent chance of heading off trouble before it becomes serious.

Holding a Grudge

Do you have a tendency to evaluate people today on the basis of what they did yesterday? A lot of us do. If your boss continues to bring up a mistake you made last week, last month, or last year, you can very politely remind him that although you made a mistake, it won't happen again, and what's past is past. This is just one more aspect of "managing" your boss.

Now make certain you don't undermine your own subordinates in the same way. If you are going to keep harping on their past mistakes, you may as well fire them right away, because you're giving them no chance to redeem themselves. Once more it is a matter of wearing one hat, of treating your subordinates just as you would like your boss to treat you.

We were having a meeting one day with a number of our key

executives. We had tentatively agreed to send Michael, a member of our firm, to represent a number of our clients at the Cannes Film Festival. But one of my associates interjected, "Hey, not so fast. Do you remember the way he screwed up at Cannes when he was there three or four years ago?"

"I remember it very well," I said. "I also remember how many assignments Michael has handled brilliantly since that time. My memory is good, and I remember situations that you and I and all of us have screwed up in recent years, too. None of us live in glass houses. Let's evaluate in terms of the present, not the past."

We finally agreed that Michael should be given another chance, and he took off for Paris the following week en route to the film festival. We heard nothing but praise from our clients about Michael, "our man in Cannes." Remember to evaluate your associates in terms of today, not yesterday.

Many of us tend to be overcritical of our business associates. We constantly point out the mistakes they make and the faux pas they commit. I certainly don't overlook the mistakes and the faux pas, but I don't harp on them. We're all just human beings. None of us behaves in an exemplary fashion one hundred percent of the time.

I evaluate everyone in our organization. Once I have established that the good outweighs the bad, I excuse their transgressions. As the man from Nazareth said some two thousand years ago, "He who is without sin among ye, let him cast the first stone." I have "sinned"—who hasn't? I make mistakes constantly, but I have remained successful in the business world for many years because I do more things right than I do wrong. If I evaluate myself that way, then it is only proper for me to evaluate others in the same terms. Woody Allen said it in a different way. "To be successful," he said, "you just have to show up half the time." Woody Allen goes too far, of course, but it is pointless and self-defeating to hold grudges against people who make mistakes or who occasionally act in an unprofessional manner.

We had a crisis in our office recently. One of our young executives, Clarence, became so distressed about an office situation that he had an emotional outburst and walked out of the office in mid-afternoon. The next morning he didn't show up. He called in sick. Later it was determined that he had gone on an alcoholic binge and hadn't come to the office the following day because he had had a hangover.

What to do? Fire him? Give him twenty lashes? Scold him? Reprimand him? I decided on another tactic. "Tell me all about it," I said.

"About what?" he replied. It was obvious that he was going to try to brazen it out.

It took me a half hour before I was able to get him to open up. He just couldn't stand the pressure of a particular situation. He finally exploded and went berserk. As I listened to his story, I felt great sympathy for him. Many people react to stressful situations in the same manner. I react differently. I sulk, get snappish, sarcastic, bitter, but I remain in control. Yet I can understand the person who blows up. I don't accept the late Harry Truman's adage, "If you can't stand the heat, stay out of the kitchen." My philosophy is that if the kitchen occasionally gets too hot for you, walk out for a while until you cool off. Then go back in.

I counseled with Clarence. I suggested that he try not to get so upset about the crises that beset any business environment. If he felt that he couldn't control his emotions, he should take a walk around the block for half an hour. If that didn't calm him down, he should take the rest of the day off. "But tell your secretary where you're going so that we don't worry about you," I said, "and don't go off on a drunken binge. You'll only feel worse in the morning, not better—as you've already found out."

Clarence accepted my advice in good spirits. He appreciated the fact that I understood what had happened to him, and that I had admonished him not for his problem but for the manner in which he had handled it. Clarence will have other outbursts, but his overall performance is of such a high caliber that I accept him for what he is. I don't hold a grudge against Clarence. He's not perfect, but none of us is.

ROGERS' RULES FOR GRUDGES

1. Don't bring up old errors unless they recur.

2. Trust your people, just as you expect your boss to trust you. Trust involves a certain degree of risk, but if you are not willing to take certain risks, then you shouldn't be a manager.

3. Expect excellence, not perfection. Expecting perfection will have the entire office walking on eggshells—the perfect climate for mistakes to occur.

Improving the Performance of Your Subordinates

You must be something of a psychologist to motivate your people to constantly improve their performance. The key is to find the trigger, or triggers, that will encourage them to try to do better and better and better.

What do your subordinates care about? You won't find the answer at staff meetings—each person's needs, ambitions, and motivations are different. If you are genuinely interested in discovering what is important to a subordinate, a series of individual meetings—not formalized sessions—is the key to discovery. You will find that by digging and probing you will find the switch that turns each person on. You may complain that you don't have the time to treat your people as individuals. That may be so, but then you had better find a way to improve performance other than working through your people—and I don't have the slightest idea what that might be.

Find the Key

There is a misconception that people are interested only in money. This isn't true. Money is important up to a point, but in most cases money is just a way to keep score. As journalist Katherine Whitehorn writes, "Money to a businessman is what rank is to a soldier, billing is to an actress, or a lectureship in a prestigious department is to an academic. More money means that a person is appreciated, that he enjoys a particular position in the company, and that he is paid as much as, or more than his peers. The money itself, the actual dollars, constitute only a small part of this motivation." Ditto for titles. There may be fifteen hundred vice-presidents in a company, but everyone wants the title because it sets him apart from the fifteen thousand other employees who don't have one. It puts him a step above.

While you are talking to each one of your people to find out what turns him or her on, you will no doubt discover one common denominator: everyone wants to be rewarded for doing a good job. I agree with Michael Le Boeuf, professor of management at the University of New Orleans, who states that "the greatest management principle in the world" is "reward people for the right behavior, and you get the right results; fail to reward the right behavior and you're likely to get the wrong results."

You must make certain that your people are rewarded for extra efforts *and* extra results. Everyone wants performance to be related to rewards, and if you are in a position to give your people rewards, it is imperative that you do so. What rewards? What is important to your people? Once you have determined that, then it should not be too difficult for you to allocate different rewards to different employees. If you are not yet in a management position where you can offer rewards to your people, recommend to your boss that he institute such a program.

I have already mentioned money and titles as possible rewards, but let's go on to other incentives:

1. Time off over and above the normal vacation period.
2. More of what they like to do and less of what they don't like to do.
3. An announcement in the presence of their peers that a job was particularly well done.
4. More freedom—more authority—more autonomy.
5. Prizes. They can take the form of dinner with spouse and children, tickets to sporting events, or a weekend at a nearby resort.
6. Educational opportunities. Some of your employees might be seeking new educational opportunities at university extension programs. Offer to pay their tuitions.

You will find that the reward system will work for you. Let me quote Michael Le Boeuf once more. "The most important point to remember is this: you aren't managing people; you're leading them. Once you set up a positive reward system for achieving the right goals, people quickly become their own best managers. And that means more time and freedom for you—a pretty good reward in itself."

Is There a Reason Why You Cannot Motivate?

Of course, you may face the problem that as hard as you try, you cannot motivate your employees to perform beyond their present capabilities. There may be many reasons for this, and I will not try to go into them. But I have repeatedly seen cases where the middle manager's lack of ability to inspire improved performance stems from an obscure cause: he has consciously or unconsciously improved his own performance, but he has not imparted his newly acquired talents and know-how to his subordinates. He has developed a new set of work rules for himself and assumes that his associates will pick up his new rules by osmosis or instinct. It doesn't work that way—he hasn't taught them how to play this new game. He suddenly finds himself disenchanted with the team that he had so carefully trained a year or two before, and he can't understand what has happened to them. Nothing has happened to them; they're the same. But he has changed. He has improved his own performance, but he has not taken his subordinates up the ladder of achievement with him.

SARAH'S STORY

I am reminded of the time that a disconsolate Sarah walked into my office, stood at my desk, and almost woefully said, "May I interrupt you for a few minutes? I really need to talk to you."

Sarah was one of our best group supervisors. She had four account executives reporting to her, and I had long believed that she ran one of the most efficient operations in our company. I quickly stood up and replied, "Of course, Sarah, sit down. I'll close the door and then we can talk privately." I sat in an upholstered chair opposite the couch where Sarah had seated herself. "Okay now, tell me what's bothering you."

Sarah told me her problem. She was dissatisfied with the performance of her staff. They had worked together as a harmonious team for more than a year, and although she was not aware of any client dissatisfaction, she did not feel that they were performing up to the standards that she had set for herself and for them.

"I don't understand it," she mused. "I try to motivate them as I always have in the past, but I feel as though I'm pushing a truck up a mountain."

I sensed what the problem might be, because I knew that Sarah had enhanced her own public relations skills in recent years, and I had been thinking that she was ready to take on added responsibilities. I decided to pursue my hunch.

"Sarah, haven't you and your team worked together for more than a year?"

"Yes, we have."

"Have you always been dissatisfied with them?" I asked.

"No, to the contrary," she replied. "A year ago I praised them singly and together all the time, and told them that we were the best group in Rogers and Cowan."

"Well, if they were that good a year ago, what happened to them that makes you so dissatisfied with them today?"

She looked at me, smiled ruefully, and said, "I don't know. That's why I'm here talking to you. I was hoping you could come up with some answers for me."

"Maybe I can," I said. "Let's talk about you for a minute. Do you know what's happened to you during the past year?"

"No, what's happened to me? I have no idea what you're referring to."

"I think you will once I've reminded you," I countered. "You're not the same person you were a year ago. You've learned a great deal about public relations in general and our business specifically in the past year. You have greater skills, broader knowledge, and you are a much better public relations practitioner than you used to be."

"Thanks, Henry, I've worked very hard at improving my performance. I didn't think you had noticed, but what has that got to do with the subject we've been discussing?"

"Yes, I've noticed," I replied, "and it has everything to do with your dissatisfaction. Let me explain. A year ago you were driving along at forty miles an hour and your team drove along with you at the same speed. Today you're driving at seventy-five miles an hour and your team is still driving at forty miles an hour. You've left them behind. Your standards are higher but you haven't communicated to them that you've changed the rules. There is nothing wrong with the people who work for you. You're the problem."

We discussed her situation for half an hour. Sarah had been listening intently. Suddenly a smile lit up her face. "Damn it, I think you're right," she exclaimed. "How could I have been so stupid?" She jumped up and started to pace back and forth.

"Of course," she continued. "It's not them. It's me. I've gotten better in my job, my standards are higher, and I just expect more from them than I did a year ago. But I have no right to expect more. I assumed that we were all growing and learning together, but we weren't. I left them behind and now I have to help them catch up."

Sarah stopped pacing. She looked at me. "Thanks," she said, "you really made me understand my problem. I don't know why I wasn't able to figure that out myself. Now I've really got my work cut out for me."

We talked many times after that on the same subject, and after six months she told me that she was once more satisfied with the performance of her subordinates.

Giving Credit Where Credit Is Due

A thousand times a day in every office, in every company, in every factory in the country, the same complaint is voiced by employees about the boss. "He's always criticizing me. He's always picking on me, but he never gives me credit for the good things I do." As an employer I know that their complaints are often justified, and knowing the sensitivities of employees on this subject, I sometimes give praise to those who are doing a routinely good job—the job that they are being paid for.

Too often, however, the employer overlooks the opportunity to praise one of his subordinates when he does a job "above and beyond the call of duty." That's when you should give a bow, an accolade to one of your employees. Examples of "above and beyond" are with us every day:

- Working overtime without overtime pay, in order to get a job completed.
- Working on a weekend to get a report done before Monday morning.
- Solving a problem that has perplexed everyone else.
- Handling an assignment that brings approval from the customer or the client.
- Handling an assignment that brings profit to the company.
- Taking on an added assignment voluntarily that is not part of normal job responsibilities.
- Helping an associate.
- Acting as a leader, rallying the troops to do a better job.

Mark Goodson, one of the television industry's most distinguished personages, has this to say about giving credit: "I've long realized that credit is as important as money. That's especially true in television. At Goodson-Todman, when we pilot a new show, there are some twenty-five different people involved, from the executive producer at the top down to the lowliest production assistant. I make it a point when the pilot is finished to write a personal letter to each of these people thanking them for their contribution.

"In addition, if someone works on a show that *doesn't* pan out, I go out of my way to send that person a note complimenting him or her on the *effort*, with a copy to the rest of the staff."

Making Them Feel Important

Each of your employees feels a sense of pride and self-esteem if you are doing your job properly as his boss. You must give each person in your group your undivided attention when you are meeting with him. You must actually believe that he is important. You can't fake it. If you can get this point across, you are going to get greater performances from him. In contrast, when an individual's self-esteem is deflated, his level of energy and performance is decreased.

Each manager and each executive has his own style and his own way of activating this theme. Dr. Sidney Harman, president of Harman International and a noted authority on "work humanization," offers the following:

"I really don't think so much in terms of making people feel important as I do in terms of making them feel genuinely respected. For example, at JBL (the makers of some of the finest high-quality audio speaker systems in the world) we have over the years conducted "open house" visits by the families of all the people working in the factory. The open house has been a gala affair, including lunch and entertainments on the lawn, but most important have been the tours through the factory where workers can demonstrate their work to their families. In that demonstration is the essence of what you call "important" because the employee makes it very clear to the family that if he were not doing this critical job, the wonderful end product would not result.

"We don't have much taste for badges, watches—that sort of stuff. We do it because it is so traditional, but our emphasis is on creating an environment of genuine mutual respect between the managers and the managed. Thus, we have started a cost-savings sharing program in which the employees and managers agree on mutually acceptable production levels, and savings beyond those levels which are generated through greater productivity are shared equitably between the company and the employees. In many ways, we find this arrangement better than traditional profit-sharing because the factory workers are not placed in the position where they may be doing marvelous work—only to discover that management has them manufacturing Edsels."

You know how you respond when someone makes you feel important. Your employees respond in the same manner, and just to prove the point I will illustrate my reaction when someone makes me feel important.

Robert Altman, of Clifford & Warnke, is our Washington attorney. When I telephone for an appointment, his secretary always asks if they can send a car to pick me up at the Dulles Airport. After I have had my meeting with him, he always asks if he can have his car and driver take me back to my hotel. Would I ever think of getting another Washington lawyer?

There are thousands of restaurants in New York. I keep gravitating back to the 21 Club. Why? They make me feel important. When I walk in, three different greeters meet me at the door with an effusive, "Hello, Mr. Rogers. Glad to have you back." One takes my coat and checks it for me, another takes my briefcase and tucks it away, returning it to me before I leave.

When I approach the dining room, I look above the cash register and see *Rogers' Rules for Success* on display among the books. As I approach the dining room, Sheldon Tannen, Pete Kriendler, or Jerry Berns (the owners) greet me and usually make a complimentary remark about the suit or shirt I'm wearing. Walter, the maitre d', shakes my hand and ushers me to a table. If I'm with a woman friend, Mario brings over a white or red carnation and puts it on the table in front of her. Why would I ever want to go to another New York restaurant?

When you make a person feel important, he is willing to extend himself just a bit further, and there is a good chance that his level of performance will skyrocket.

Encouragement and Recognition

It is your responsibility as an employer, a manager, a supervisor to get the highest possible performance from the people who report to you. Compare yourself to a football coach. You guide, you counsel, you advise, you teach, you inspire—you encourage. You can't walk away. You cannot ignore. If you do, you are abdicating your responsibility, and at that point your own performance is in question.

Encouragement is another sensitive issue, because there are many bosses who ignore the difference between imposing and intervening. Imposing your will on an employee doesn't work, and it breeds resentment, because you're saying, "Here, let me show you. Do it my way." That will not bring you the results you are after. Intervening, on the other hand, means *guiding*, helping, pointing your employee in the right direction. Your objective is to get the job done and get it done efficiently. There is no reason why he should do it your way. There are a dozen ways to achieve the same objective. You must steer him to find the way that is right for him.

Remember that your encouragement must have an objective. Usually the objective is improved performance. I remember the story often told about Henry Kissinger during his years as secretary of state. He had developed a way of encouraging his subordinates to a higher performance level with a very simple tactic. Whenever one of his associates placed a document on his desk for approval, he would read it quickly and then return it with a cryptic note that read "You can do it better." Invariably, when the paper was returned to him it was better than it was the first time. I don't advocate such an approach, even though that form of encouragement paid off for Mr. Kissinger.

In contrast, let me tell you some of the things I do to encourage my associates:

- When an article on one of our associates appears in print, I put a copy of it on our bulletin board and send additional copies to our offices in New York, Washington, and London.
- When a letter addressed to me from one of our clients praises the work of one of our associates, it receives similar distribution throughout the organization.
- I am a strong advocate of giving vice-president titles to our associates. It gives them an added stature with the clients they represent and with the media, and it enhances their own self-images.
- When I write to a client, I always use the pronoun "we," and in most instances I use the name of the person or persons who are involved with that client.
- When I meet with a client and one of my associates, I always let my associate take the lead in the conversation. I feel that it is important for him or her to make the impression, not me.

Understanding

Have you forgotten some of the mistreatment you received before you achieved the middle management rank? Don't fall for the old cliché, "My boss gave me ulcers—now it's my turn to give them to the people who work for me."

Avoid setting up a boss-employee relationship; playing an authoritative role establishes a we-they relationship. Drawing a line between you and your employee inhibits productive work relationships. That doesn't mean you should hide your strength. If someone's work is unsatisfactory you must speak up, but you must show understanding and consideration.

I like to think of myself as a helpful friend. We're all on the same team, and although every team needs a captain, the captain should also be a friend.

Fred Bucy, former president of Texas Instruments, has some observations on being an effective boss that I found fascinating. He says:

"It doesn't take much talent to issue orders. It does take continued discipline to study the variety of people you are leading in order to understand what it takes to motivate them and to inspire them to do their very best to make the company and themselves a success. Also, it is a never-ending task to be an effective leader, because time changes all things. What might work at one point in time will not work at another point in time; e.g., what would work in the sixties would not work in the seventies. What was effective in the seventies is not effective in the eighties. Therefore, you must discipline yourself to keep up with changing values.

"It takes one set of leadership skills to motivate a manager with many years of experience and another to motivate young people just arriving from universities. Also, what is effective in motivating a person at one point in his career will not be effective in motivating him later; an individual's values change depending upon what is happening in his personal life as well as his success with his career. Therefore, one of the most important things that a boss or leader must do is to continue to study how to be effective. This does take discipline. It is much easier to assume that what worked yesterday will work today, and that is simply not true."

Acting as a Role Model

An effective boss does talk about performance. He leads by example. Again I quote Donald E. Peterson, who says, "Of course it's what we *do* that counts, not what we say. Therefore I set an example through my actions and I believe it is critically important to be consistent, predictable, and dependable."

Your image with your subordinates is dependent on many factors—knowledge, personal credibility, self-respect, and sound work habits, among others. In your present position you can't stand still, and you must constantly set an example for those who report to you.

When I asked Harold Burson, chairman of Burson-Marstellar, the largest public relations organization in the world, what his views were on being a role model for his employees, he said, "I simply act naturally the way I have always acted. I am in the office at seven-thirty, I work most weekends."

As a middle manager you must remember that you are in the spotlight. Your employees are watching you, and their good or bad performance is directly related to yours.

ROGERS' RULES FOR IMPROVING THE PERFORMANCE OF YOUR SUBORDINATES

1. Most people can improve their performance level if they are coached, taught, led. You can't always turn a bad employee into a good one, but sometimes all it takes is pushing the right button or ringing the right bell.

2. Expectations create their own reality. Maintain a positive attitude about the capabilities and improvement potential of your team members.

3. Everyone will not improve, but when everyone is given the opportunity to improve, those who can't make it eventually fall by the wayside.

4. Share. Impart your newly acquired knowledge to your subordinates and to your boss too.

5. Be a brain picker, and encourage your subordinates to be the same.

6. For your subordinates to grow, they must be encouraged to disagree, and not be expected to carry out your orders obediently. Your subordinates must be brought about, not ordered around.

7. Act as a role model to your employees.

2

Building a Winning Team

If your quarterback is playing by one set of rules and your right tackle by another, you're not going to win too many games. If your halfback complains that the guards aren't moving fast enough for him and if your right end refuses to work with your left end, then the defense will have a field day. Sports analogies for business situations have become almost a cliché, but the truth is that the conditions really are quite similar.

Even though you are in middle management, you're the captain of your own team, and your effectiveness is directly related to the quality of people who play on the team and how smoothly they work together. In the last chapter, we talked about how to improve individual performance. Now let's examine how to build coordination and team spirit among your players.

Building Effective Relationships

What are your relationships with the members of your team? Although it depends in some measure on whether your team consists of people you hired or people you "inherited," I can hear most of you out there saying, "Oh, I get along great with my staff. A few ups and downs here and there, maybe, but on the whole I have wonderful personal and professional relationships with the people who report to me." You may be kidding yourself.

Unfortunately, we don't see ourselves as others see us, and I am sure you would be shocked to learn the truth about what the members of your team really think of their captain. You would be surprised if you were to see the results of a confidential poll taken of your people about you. A few people would give you a one hundred percent rating. Some would be passive; their attitude would be, "Uh, he's alright." Others would say they were not in a position to evaluate you because they really don't know you. Some would say you were warm and friendly, others would say you were cold, distant, aloof. Some would like you. Some would dislike you.

If you agree that there might be some truth to my prognosis, and if you are like most middle management people, you would find that the persons who gave you the highest ratings were the few selected people with whom you enjoy close relationships. They comprise your Inner Circle; they are the rare stars in your firmament. With the rest of your staff you probably have no relationship at all, or at best a strained and formal one.

If you do have an Inner and an Outer Circle, and if you agree that this is not a healthy condition, how do you fix it? I won't pretend that it's easy, but you must attempt to break down the wall between yourself and the outer circle. Your ultimate objective should be to obliterate the difference between the two.

The first step is to identify whether or not the two groups actually exist. Don't depend entirely on your own opinion. You are not objective. You cannot see the group that comprises your team as they see themselves in relation to you, their leader. Have a talk with a number of your subordinates and get a reading. Think carefully about who you will talk with. Try to select a cross section. Pick a few people with whom you have a close relationship and a few who you don't know well at all. Whether or not you get truthful, candid answers to your questions is directly related to the manner in which you approach the interview. Take off your executive's hat. Get out from behind your desk. Offer your employee a cup of coffee. Get into your most relaxed position and encourage him to do the same. Are you ready? Here is your opening line:

"I have a problem and I need your advice."

Each one of the people you have selected for this quiz session will have the same reaction: "Wow!" Each one of them will think, "The boss is asking *me* for advice. I wonder what's going on."

They will be suspicious, they will be cautious, but you're halfway home in getting honest answers from them because they are flattered and pleased that *you* are asking them for advice. From that point on you must gently lead them on with a list of questions and observations that will give you the information you are seeking. Here are some examples:

"I would like *us* to build a stronger team and I'm talking with you because I consider you to be one of the key players."

"How do you think we can improve our team performance? Do you believe that some people on our team get better treatment than others?" (*Caution*—don't mention Inner or Outer Circles. That's the equivalent of waving a red flag.)

"Do you believe we should have more frequent staff meetings?"

"Do you feel that the conduct of staff meetings can be improved?"

By asking indirect questions such as these, you will learn what each of your people is thinking, whether he believes that Inner and Outer Circles exist, and who he thinks are the individuals on each team. Then, when you receive an indication of their opinion, try to pinpoint your own. Take a good hard look at your team. Is there someone who hides every time he sees you coming? Is there someone *you* hide from every time you see *him* coming? Who do you really like? Who do you dislike? Once you have established that potentially dangerous Inner and Outer Circles do exist, then it is time to take action. You must build relationships with everyone on your team.

To build relationships, you must prepare to spend time with those you don't know and those you have decided you don't like. This won't be easy, but being an effective manager never is. Think about how this situation came about—why you don't know them, why you don't like them. Have you been hasty or unfair? Maybe they're not so bad after all. You must put your judgments aside and try to get to know them as well as you do those you have decided are your superstars.

It's easy for me to tell you what to do. It's not so easy for you to do it. No one ever taught you how to build effective relationships in the business world.

An excellent approach is presented in the recently published book, *Managing for Excellence,* by David L. Bradford and Allan R. Cohen. They put you on the right track when they say, "Put your arm around your subordinate and draw the person close." Here is a person you have ignored up until now. Now I ask you to put your arm around him—figuratively speaking, of course. Your objective should be to get to know and understand this man or woman as well as you do those who are members of your Inner Circle.

How do you put your arm around him? What is the first step?

How do you get to know him? First, without making a great point of it, spread your choice assignments among your staff members more democratically than you have in the past. It is only natural that your "favorites" have been receiving preferred treatment when it has been time to allocate assignments. Now that your objective is to make everyone on the team a "favorite," begin to give the most interesting new challenges to those who had previously been members of the Outer Circle.

Now is the time to think of the Power of Lunch. Food is the great icebreaker, the great equalizer. Everyone gets hungry; everyone eats. Your secretary, your co-worker, your boss, and the chairman of the board all must take nourishment just like you do, and most people dislike eating alone.

ROGERS' RULES FOR GIVING GOOD LUNCH

1. Ask a member of the Outer Circle to lunch. He may be apprehensive, but assure him in advance that it will be a good, upbeat lunch.

2. Start by telling the truth—that you want to build a stronger staff and that the first step is to get closer to everyone who works with you. Assure him that he isn't being singled out, that others will follow.

3. Don't expect too much the first time. Your lunch "date" may be suspicious; he may doubt your sincerity. That is the price you have to pay for having neglected him. It might take two meetings, or three, or six.

4. Be sincere. Your concern about establishing a new relationship must be genuine. You don't have to like him, but you must try to understand him, his likes and dislikes, his goals and aspirations.

5. Proceed through the rest of your team. You will probably find that the news of the "lunch campaign" has preceded you and that the rest of the group isn't as apprehensive or suspicious as their predecessor was.

6. Make certain you don't forget anyone. The resultant wail of "The boss took everyone in the department to lunch but me" will echo in the corridors and the bad vibrations will reverberate for a long, long time.

7. Let your boss know what you're doing. He will most likely give you a vote of confidence. There's some chance that he will scoff and say that your plan isn't worth all the effort. If that occurs, ignore it; you and I know better. And there's always the chance that he will be so impressed with what you are doing he will adopt your program for himself. I'll bet that if he does, you will be the first person he invites to lunch.

Building a Team That Works Together

I've said it before; I'll say it again. It's not easy. Nothing about being a successful middle manager is easy, and as you move higher and higher up the ladder, it gets more difficult all the time. Don't be so quick to envy your boss. You think he has it made. The fact is that he is having a tougher time than you are, and his problems are less formidable than his boss's.

One of your greatest responsibilities is to build a team that works together. If they do, you can take a small part of the credit; if they don't you must assume one hundred percent of the blame. One of the least pleasant tasks a middle manager must undertake is to get people to put individual differences aside in the interest of getting the work done. Even as you can't expect to like everyone on your team, you can't expect them all to like each other. It is sufficient that they can work together and be civil, if not cordial, face to face. It's unreasonable to think that Jim will greet Roger warmly when you know he is sure that Roger is bucking for his job. Your job is to maintain a working truce during office hours, and to do so without appearing to take sides.

It is up to you to get your people, not necessarily to like each other, but to agree to work with each other during office hours. You must explain to each of them how harmful it is to the department and to the entire business for them to remain at swords' points. Their response will depend upon your relationship with them. If you have built that relationship since the first day you started to work with them, and they feel a loyalty to both you and the company, they will try to be team players. If you have no or little relationship with them, you have your job cut out for you.

You cannot motivate people through mass appeal. You cannot motivate people by staff meetings. You cannot motivate people by sending out memos "to our staff." It doesn't work. To repeat— you have to do it one to one. It takes a lot of time and a lot of effort, but it pays off.

You must also understand that everyone is not motivated in the same way. Each of your employees is probably motivated by something different. Some people require a strong, aggressive approach. Other people must be handled in a more sensitive manner. You will be an effective manager when you are able to distinguish between the different types of people who work for you and devise a motivational approach for each type with whom you have to deal.

Trying to build a team that works together can be a frustrating experience, and you must expect to have many disappointments on the way. Despite your best efforts, there will be times when you get kicked in the teeth. You will say to yourself, "I'm knocking myself out to build this team, but no one appreciates me."

ROGERS' RULES FOR BUILDING A TEAM THAT WORKS TOGETHER

1. Treat your subordinates equally, thereby setting an example for what their own behavior should be.

2. Let them know that "divide and conquer" tactics won't work with you.

3. Let them know that you, as their boss, absolutely disapprove of backbiting on your team.

Don't be disturbed if, despite your best efforts, someone remains a troublemaker, a non-team player, and continues to be responsible for dissension on your team. This is particularly annoying and frustrating if that person is more talented than many of your other team members. You won't like to read this, but my advice is to figure out a way to get rid of him. He's talented, yes, but he also destroys morale, keeps everyone in a constant state of anger and resentment, and worst of all, gives you constant sleepless nights.

I was faced with just such a problem. A new associate came on board about a year ago, and quickly proved to be a powerhouse, the kind of person we rarely find in our business. Peter brought new clients to the firm, related well to the other clients we had assigned him to, and worked long hours in a totally professional manner. There was only one problem. From the day he joined our firm, there seemed to be a new personnel crisis every day. Peter refused to work with Bill. Peter couldn't get along with Dick. Peter had a rip-roaring argument with Janice. The time had come for a talk with Peter. I walked into his office one afternoon.

"Do you have a few minutes?" I asked.

"Sure, what's up?" Peter replied.

"You're doing a great job for us, Peter, and I want you to know how much I appreciate everything you've accomplished in recent months. That's why it's so difficult for me to bring up this unpleasant situation."

Peter sat up straight in his chair. He seemed to bristle. "What situation?"

"I hear you're causing problems among other people in the office."

"That's not true," he replied angrily. "They're causing the problems, not me."

Peter went on to explain that he was willing to work with and cooperate with everyone. They had rejected him. They refused to work with him. He was working under tremendous pressures because he was receiving no cooperation from his colleagues. His tirade against other staff members went on for ten minutes.

"It's interesting," I said finally, "that the very people you are railing about don't seem to have problems with anyone else. Why would they have all selected you for their vendettas?"

"I have no idea," he replied, "but I decided that that's their problem, not mine. You just told me that I was doing a great job for the company; that's all that matters."

I left Peter's office feeling that I had accomplished nothing. We never see ourselves as others see us, I thought to myself. Peter doesn't realize that doing a great job was not all that mattered if the morale of a half-dozen other team players was destroyed in the process.

We continued to discuss Peter and the problem for a number of months after that meeting. We talked to Peter and his associates many times. There was no improvement in his relationships. We talked about discharging him but we didn't want to do that. Peter, despite the problems he caused, was too valuable. We were in a quandary.

Peter finally solved the problem for us. One day he did something that management felt was improper. If someone else had done it, we would have allowed it to pass by with only a slight reprimand. With Peter, in contrast, we took a hard line. Peter was indignant; he submitted his resignation the same day. We accepted it. By the end of the week he was gone.

It took a lot of scurrying around to keep our house in order. We had to pick up the pieces that Peter had left behind. We had to assure the clients with whom he was involved that they would continue to be well represented, and we immediately began to look for a replacement. Fortunately, a top-level person became available, and within a few weeks order was restored.

I faced another frustrating experience a few years ago when we were getting ready to move our offices. We were moving to larger quarters and beginning to think about who would occupy which offices. Who would get the more desirable window offices? When we had moved ten years before, we were still small enough that Warren Cowan and I could personally decide who would go where. Now we were a larger organization, and we decided it was no longer proper for us to face the almost guaranteed criticism that would come if we were to autocratically decide on office assignments. Let democracy reign! Let the troops decide for themselves.

We selected a space planning committee comprised of representative members of each of our departments. All of the one hundred twenty-five employees in our Los Angeles offices were represented so their interests would be protected. Very smug because we thought we had headed off a controversial situation, we sent out a memo outlining the plan, which named the members of the space planning committee. The following day I found a sealed envelope on my desk marked PRIVATE AND CONFIDENTIAL. In it was a copy of the memo, overprinted in bold red pencil: *"I don't believe you guys!"* Then a *"F*** You"* and other profanities and the accusation that this was all a phony plot conceived by the partners to take the heat off themselves, that they and the other "sacred cows" in the organization would wind up in plush quarters while the "peasants" would once more be relegated to unlit, airless cubicles.

I was annoyed and disappointed. I felt that our intentions did not call for a four-letter-worded response. I became dejected and frustrated, and remained in that state of mind until I reminded myself that there are always dissidents and rebels in any organization. I called a meeting of our executive committee and passed around the anonymous message. For a few minutes we all tried to analyze the handwriting to figure out who the disgruntled Trotskyite could be, but we finally gave up.

Was the space planning committee a phony? Had we positioned the Inner Circle on the committee, leaving the "peasants" out in the cold? No. We had made a point of not doing that. The space planning committee was representative of the entire staff. After much soul-searching we decided we had done our best and had come up with the space allocation plan that would please the largest number of people, but obviously we had not succeeded with everyone. As a manager you should realize that despite your best efforts, you're not going to satisfy all of your people all of the time. Expect occasional disappointments.

Losing the Battle and Winning the War

If building a winning team is really important to you, then you must learn to lose an occasional battle so that you can win the war. Let me explain. We all like to win. We all like to prove our superiority. But if you ever tried to evaluate what you actually gained when you won a battle and what you forfeited when you lost, you would be surprised to discover that often the losses are wins and the wins are losses.

Your responsibility is to get peak performance out of your team. To accomplish this, your players must like you, they must respect and admire you, and they must be inspired to work like hell so that they and you both look good.

What do you gain when you prove one of your associates to be wrong? Nothing. For a moment you may feel smug and superior. You may say to yourself, "I guess I showed him who the boss is around here!" But have you thought about what is going on in your employee's mind at the same moment? He is probably saying to himself. "He is a S.O.B. He just had to win every discussion. He'll never admit that I'm right. I backed down because he's my boss. If he weren't, I'd argue the point until kingdom come. God damn it, I'm mad as hell." Is that the way to build a team?

You must let your colleagues win some of the battles, because it is essential that they retain their self-respect. To many of your subordinates, losing face in any situation is a devastating experience. Here is another situation where you must put yourself in the other person's shoes. How would you feel if your boss insisted on winning in every discussion in which you had a difference of opinion? Maybe you don't have a boss like that. If you do, you know what I mean. You resent him, and resentment is not a healthy attitude for any member of a team to have. You should treat your employees as you would like your boss to treat you. Remember, that's the heart of the one-hat solution.

Disagreements between you and members of your staff are healthy. They are a sign of a mutually respectful relationship. You should not wrestle your employee to the mat to prove him wrong. At one point you should back down and let him save face. Look at him when you say, "Okay, let's try it your way." The expression of triumph on his face must make you realize that you are really the winner. You have lost this skirmish, but you have added one more layer of muscle to the strength of your team.

ROGERS' RULES FOR RUNNING A HAPPY SHOP

1. Impress upon your subordinates the importance of working together as a team. Accomplish this by meeting them one on one.

2. Be visible to your teammates and make certain that they know you are there to help them. Let them know you have an open-door policy and welcome their calls or personal visits at any time.

3. Make certain that priorities are clear to everyone. Everyone must know specifically what his responsibilities are, what you expect of him, and when you expect it.

4. Your team should have specific goals; they should know what the goals are and what the rewards will be if they achieve them.

5. Praise individual team members for individual accomplishments, and make both the accomplishments and the praise known to other members on the team.

6. If a team member deserves criticism, it should be given to him in private, and he should be told that the subject is a closed one known only to you and him.

7. Spot potential problems and personality clashes before they happen by being sensitive to anything unusual that happens around you. Have eyes in the back of your head and listen carefully for rumors of impending internecine strife.

8. If you discover a feud involving two of your team members, step in and handle it quickly. Your responsibility is to make peace.

Preventing "The Peter Principle"

Dr. Lawrence Peter won acclaim in the corporate world a number of years ago with an insightful book entitled *The Peter Principle*. He has written a number of successful books since then, and his principle has placed him in the Business Hall of Fame for all eternity.

THE PETER PRINCIPLE:
"In a hierarchy an employee tends to be elevated to his level of incompetence."

I devoured *The Peter Principle* avidly when it was first published, because from the moment I first read the principle itself I knew that Dr. Peter had written it just for me. For many years I had been guilty of elevating my employees to their level of incompetence. Some examples:

I had elevated a top secretary in our New York office to office manager. The result was disastrous. She was a great secretary. She was a terrible office manager.

I had asked an excellent account executive in our television department to become head of the department. He protested, "I'm not an executive." "You can be," I replied. "Just try and I'll help you." He tried and I tried, but it didn't work. We returned him to his former position. Now he's happy and I am, too.

One of the biggest problems that every manager faces is the common practice of promoting within the ranks or even hiring someone from outside to fill a position that he is not qualified to handle. It happens to all of us, so if you recognize that you have such a problem, don't chastise yourself. You're not alone. Join the club. The problem is, what are you going to do about it?

Managers often make the mistake of placing a person in a position of responsibility and authority before the person is ready. Then they compound the first mistake by becoming impatient with what appears to be the subordinate's inability to grow into the job—his "incompetence." The person is fired and emerges somewhere else as a big success.

I've been guilty of this myself. One day, Carol walked into my office to say hello. "Hi, Henry," she said. "I'm glad to be back." Nine years after I had fired her, she was back at Rogers & Cowan as head of our television division. How did it happen?

We needed a new television head when we hired her the first time. Carol was working in a managerial position in a network publicity department when she joined us. I trained her for her new post, which involved bringing new business into the firm and supervising the representation of clients. I introduced her to prospective clients in New York. I arranged for her to meet the proper people at major ad agencies and television advertisers. I introduced her to the proper people at television production companies. I spent many hours explaining the strategies and techniques of publicizing television series and specials. I discussed the differences between handling a show for an advertiser and handling the same show for the production company.

Perhaps because I had personally taken on the "mentor" role, I was impatient. I was critical of Carol. I was thinking, "I've spent all this time teaching her. I've given her the benefit of all my years of experience. How come it isn't sinking in? Maybe she just doesn't have what it takes." I began second-guessing her, and our relationship began to deteriorate. I credit Carol with facing the issue squarely, even though I'd been trying to avoid it. We were talking one day in her tenth month with us. Carol said, "Level with me, Henry. You're not happy with me. You feel I'm not up to the job." I couldn't lie. I agreed with her, and that day we decided that she would work the two months remaining on her contract and then leave.

The day after she left she went to work for a competitor, snaring the number-two position in their television department. Nine years later they went out of business, and a week later Carol was back at Rogers & Cowan, once again head of the television department, the position she'd been fired from nine years before.

I felt that we all had lessons to learn from this experience, and I asked her to describe what had happened as she saw it. "Henry, you were enormously helpful to me," Carol began. "I learned a lot from you, but maybe I wasn't ready just then to be the top honcho in your television department. Maybe if you had had a little more patience, it might have worked out, but once you began to doubt your own decision to make me head of the department, you began to second-guess me. That, I think, was the beginning of the end for me. I needed time to mature and gain the experience that the job required. When I stepped into a lesser position at the other company, I was where I should have been at that point in my career. I grew there. I learned there, and most importantly, I gained in self-confidence and self-esteem as the years went on. I studied every trade publication, attended seminars, and really learned every aspect of the television industry. I found the time to develop my own relationships with people in advertising and production, which was essential if I was to become tops in my job. I became not only an effective salesman, which enabled me to bring new business into the firm, but also a good manager, which enabled us to do an outstanding job for our clients. Now I can say to the people who report to me. 'Your job is to make me look good, and my job is to help you make me look good.' "

I like that. It's a good credo for any manager to adopt.

Carol was never "incompetent." She was misplaced at that

particular time. I had put her in a number-one position when at that moment in her career she was only ready to take on a number-two position. We're lucky to have her back. She could have been with us for the past nine years—if I had been a more patient manager.

If one of your employees is already experiencing The Peter Principle you face a serious problem. You can demote him—put him back in the job he previously held. This rarely works. A person feels emasculated if he/she is demoted. You can discharge him. You can help find a slot for him in another department. Or you can retrain him. None of these options are pleasant to anticipate, but part of your responsibility as a boss is to face up to unpleasant tasks. The easy solution is to do nothing, to ignore the problem, to let him be. Unfortunately, that's a cop-out. You're risking the ruin of your whole department. All of your efforts to build a winning team will be meaningless because you don't have the guts to solve a cancerous problem. You must do something.

The first step is to have a talk with the person. If he is not already aware that he is a square peg in a round hole, then it is your duty to bring it to his attention. Honesty in this case is most important, but make an effort to handle this delicate situation in a sensitive manner. It is painful to tell someone that he is incapable of handling his job. Just realize that it is more painful for him than it is for you and act accordingly.

You're lucky if he offers to resign. That's the ideal situation, but it rarely happens. He should understand that you are concerned with his welfare, but he rarely does. He should also understand that even though you are concerned about him, you are also responsible for your department and that you have a boss who holds you accountable.

Your next move is to discover what his reaction is to going back to his old position. You may find that he will welcome this suggestion, for some people are more comfortable with less responsibility rather than more. If you find that he finds this idea agreeable, put it into effect immediately. It's the best solution under the circumstances. If he resists, don't push it, because if you insist, the result will be disastrous. He will be miserable, and his dissatisfaction will infect your entire department.

Your next alternative is to retrain him. It may be that he has the capability, but was thrust into his new position without the training that he should have had. There might be a way to manage this, but it is extremely difficult. It could disrupt your whole department to have him go through a training period that he should have had before he was placed in his present position. The two of you should make this decision jointly, but before proceeding you should give serious consideration as to how other players on the team are going to react.

Finally, the last alternative: termination. Sometimes there is no other recourse but to terminate a person's employment. Time and time again I have witnessed the agony experienced by management over the prospective termination of someone who is entrenched in a particular position, a victim of the Peter Principle. In our organization, we tend to vacillate about taking the final step. The power to fire gives one a frightening responsibility, but it must be faced. You, the manager, must realize that just as it is your responsibility to hire people, it is also your responsibility to discharge those who are preventing you from managing a winning team.

I have given you the scenario for what happens or should happen when you discover that a person is suffering from the Peter Principle. Your responsibility as a manager is to prevent it from happening in the first place. Promoting someone from within the ranks should be a gradual process rather than an immediate action. While the person is still in his old position, you or one of your associates must begin to help him, teach him, guide him. The person should be given added responsibility by degrees. Finally, when you and he are both satisfied that he is ready, it is time to make the announcement and have him step into his new job. This procedure is not infallible, but it will do much to alleviate the problem of the Peter Principle in your department.

ROGERS' RULES FOR GETTING RID OF DEADWOOD

1. Face up to it. You're being paid to solve the tough problems. Have a talk with the person. If he's not already aware that he's a square peg in a round hole, bring it to his attention. Try to be sensitive.

2. Consider yourself lucky if he offers to resign or requests a transfer. It's the ideal situation, but it rarely happens. Bring up the prospect of going back to his old position. If he is agreeable, move him immediately.

3. Bring up retraining if you think the situation is retrievable. Be prepared, however, for stormy times in your department. The rest of your staff will find it disruptive to have someone in training for a position he already holds. Determine how much responsibility he will be able to exercise while in training.

4. Consider termination as a last resort. Make sure the individual is aware that this might be a possibility if his work does not improve.

Going to Bat for Your People

As you sit at your desk, imagine yourself at the center of a political arena. Everyone is vying for power. The assistant vice-president is bucking for his V.P. stripes. The V.P. is maneuvering to be a senior vice-president. Look all the way up to the top and you will see the president with his eyes on the chairman's office. Now come back to where you are. You should have your eyes set on your boss's job and be figuring out how to get there. Where to start?

First, realize that a game is being played. Second, learn the rules. Third, teach yourself to play the game as best you can. You may never learn to play as well as some others in your company, but it doesn't matter. The fact that you're playing the game, while many around you are unaware that it even exists, puts you miles ahead of the pack.

There are many different versions and variations of this contest, but the one you are playing right now is "going to bat for your people." Your first objective is to seek peak performance from them. Your efforts toward this goal are not altruistic. In fact, they are selfish, and they should be. What is good for you is good for your team, your boss, and the company. Your objective must be to make your team look good. When they do, it makes you look good. If you look good to your boss, it makes him look good to his boss. At that point, everyone is a winner.

Your people will strive for peak performance if they know that you are behind them one hundred percent of the time. Let them down, and they will let you down. You must demonstrate your loyalty to them. You must show that you care about them. They should regard you as mother, father, teacher, and friend.

For some twelve years, Kathie headed up the entertainment division of our New York office. In jest, but with enormous respect, I used to call her our "mother hen." During her tenure with our company she built up a formidable team of young women who were recognized in the New York entertainment world as the best in the business.

She took mostly inexperienced people and taught them the

rudiments of promoting motion pictures, publicizing television shows, handling personalities. One had just graduated from the School of Communications at Boston University. One had been an apprentice at another public relations firm. A few of them started as secretaries and under her guidance worked themselves up to become junior publicists, and finally senior publicists.

In the New York entertainment end of the public relations business, the normal working hours of nine to five do not exist. There are premieres and press screenings of new films to be covered. If a Rogers & Cowan employee gets home by midnight she is lucky. There are cocktail receptions and dinners where the presence of public relations representatives is required. One of our people may get up at 5:00 A.M. to pick up a client at 6:30 A.M. to accompany him to "Today," "Good Morning, America," or "CBS Morning News," all of which begin at 7:00 A.M. That same day she might act as a behind-the-scenes hostess at a luncheon at the 21 Club where one of our clients is involved, and at 7:00 P.M. she may work a movie premiere at a Times Square theater, making certain that the press gets all the information they need and that the client is well served.

Do other jobs call for hours like that? I don't know of any. Yet I never heard a word of complaint from any of Kathie's people because they all knew that Kathie cared about them and was looking after their best interests. If they were tired after a long night, Kathie would tell them not to come in the next morning. If there were a number of long nights in rapid succession, Kathie would insist that they take a couple of days off and not come in. Kathie motivated them.

She would drive her management crazy, always asking for more and more on behalf of her people—money, titles, perks. Fortunately, she was an unusually talented judge of people, and it was difficult for us to deny her. She selected as protégées women who were innately talented, who had drive and ambition. Although each was different in looks and personality, each was also a potential Kathie.

Kathie rarely, if ever, asked for anything for herself. She was always asking for her people. They made her look good, and she knew it. The result: she earned the illustrious title of President—Entertainment Division, Rogers & Cowan, New York, and she was one of the highest-paid public relations executives in the country. Her salary and annual bonus were in six figures.

What has been the payoff to management as a result of Kathie's devotion to her team? A lot of clients were most appreciative of the efforts that were made on their behalf.

Kathie recently left our employ to head up her own television production company. Although we were devastated when we heard the news, we wished her well because we knew it was a constructive career move for her.

What happened to our New York office after Kathie decided to change careers? We didn't replace her. She had done her job so well, she had trained her key people so effectively, they were all so highly motivated, that her department continued to operate efficiently and successfully even without her presence.

What does all of that have to do with you? It is the ideal example of how to play the game of "going to bat for your people." You get what you want for yourself by working like hell for the people who work for you.

ROGERS' RULES FOR "GOING TO BAT FOR YOUR PEOPLE"

1. When you are convinced that your people are working at top effectiveness, go to bat for them with your boss.

2. Seek well-deserved wage increases for them, and push to

get them "perks" at least equal to those enjoyed by other departments.

3. Let them know that you are keeping the higher-ups apprised of their accomplishments.

4. If your boss is critical of their performance, ask him to criticize you, not them. Explain to him that you are responsible for the good and the bad that takes place in your department.

5. Keep an open-door policy; let your people know that you are ready to meet with them at any time.

3

Preventing Crossed Wires

"**W**hat we have here is a failure to communicate." You heard it first in *Cool Hand Luke*, and it is just as true today. We've all heard so much about the subject of communicating and its importance in business that we tend to tune out when the subject comes up. "Yeah, yeah. We gotta communicate," I can hear all of you out there saying. If you've heard it all before, how come it's not getting through? Botched communications between employer and employee is the major cause of office crises. You may not like it, but you're about to hear more about the importance of communicating. So listen out there. I'm trying to communicate.

Don't Be Deaf Between the Ears

Have you ever suspected that the people you work with are hard of hearing? I assure you that their hearing is fine, but their listening is sadly deficient. Experts say that most of us listen with only about twenty-five percent efficiency—and that's when we're paying attention. We are literally "deaf between the ears" because we don't know how to listen.

As a child, did you ever play a game called "telephone"? One kid whispered something to the next kid and so on around a table, until the last one announced what he heard, which was completely different from what the first kid had whispered. This of course shocked, amazed, and confused the kid who had sent out the first message. Back then there were giggles all around the table when they realized what had happened, and it was all very funny. Today that same game is being played right in your own office, and you don't even realize it. There's one major difference: it's no longer funny. It's dangerous to business, to your department, and to your career.

You in middle management have the very worst of it. Why? Because the guy on top and the guy on the bottom are looking to you to transmit ideas faithfully. When things go awry, who's going to get the blame? You in the middle. Communication, it is often said, is a two-way street. You as a middle manager must begin to think of yourself as a conduit for *communication*, not merely for information. Communication must flow in two directions simultaneously.

The higher up the corporate ladder you go, the more listening and less talking you should do; there is more happening below you that you need to hear about.

LISTENING

The ability to listen is an essential trait, but it is also a difficult one. You were taught to read, write, and speak, but no one ever taught you to listen. It is a subject that should be taught in grammar school. Mothers scolding their children say, "You're not listening to me." Why should the kid listen to his mother? No one ever told him that listening was important. No one ever taught him in school how to listen. It is no wonder, then, that so many people grow up without the ability to listen.

Every chief executive officer I have ever known has stressed the importance of listening as a valuable tool in running a business. Allan Cox, in his recent book, *The Making of the Achiever*, writes: "No act in all of management—save that of thinking itself—is given as much time as the spoken word. Yet no other act in all of management is as grossly underutilized as this one in which one executive speaks to another."

LISTENING AND COMPREHENDING

Listening is one thing. Comprehending is another. Absorbing into your consciousness what the other person is saying is the result of intense listening. You might try an experiment one day. After you have had a conversation with one of your subordinates, ask him to repeat back to you what was said. You will find that invariably he has missed at least half of what you discussed. This should not surprise you; I am convinced that most people in the business world listen up to only fifty percent of their capacity. What can you do about it?

If you have a hunch that your subordinates are not listening to you to the extent that they should, certain guidelines will lead you to discover whether your hunch is correct. If someone doodles on notepads, he is not giving you one hundred percent of his attention. If he has a habit of shuffling papers while you are talking, he's not listening. If he is looking out the window, he is obviously daydreaming.

It's difficult to treat people like children and say to them, "You must listen to what I am saying." It is not only difficult, it is demeaning to them as well as to you. I have developed a technique that has proven effective for me and may be helpful to you as well.

If you are talking with one person or a group and you sense that someone is not listening—stop talking! A moment or two will probably elapse before the suspect lifts his head and looks at you. It has taken him that length of time to realize that the room has gone quiet. He will look at you and wonder why you have stopped. Once the two of you are looking at each other, you should, without a reprimand or even an explanation, pick up the conversation once again. When this happens two, three, or four times, your subordinates will find themselves trying to listen to you more intently than they have in the past, for they finally realize that you know when they are or aren't listening. I suggest you try it; I am confident that it will work for you, too.

LISTENING TO YOUR SUBORDINATES

Of course, let me remind you that listening works both ways. If you believe it is important that your subordinates listen to you, then you must make a concerted effort to listen to them. Give them the respect that you expect from them. Don't doodle, don't shuffle papers, don't look dreamily out the window; give each one of your employees the intense concentration that helps the listening process. Unbeknownst to you, you may have as big a listening problem as your employees.

Many times I have heard people say, "My boss makes me furious. He never listens to what I have to say." You may never have thought about it, but not listening will lead you to the road entitled "Poor Performance." You are looking for the road called "Improved Performance." Learning to listen to your employees will help you to find it.

LISTENING TO YOUR BOSS

Listening to your subordinates is important, but listening to your boss is doubly important. We have talked about communicating. When he talks to you or with you, he is trying to communicate, but he won't be able to do so unless you give him one hundred percent of your attention. You think you're brighter than your employees. Then accept the fact that your boss feels that he is brighter than you are.

He will quickly spot whether or not you're listening to what he says. Hearing without listening can often get you in trouble. You will not comprehend what he is asking you to do, and you will have created a problem that should never have happened. It is essential that you listen carefully and try to comprehend everything your boss is saying.

ROGERS' RULES ON LISTENING

1. Tune in. Blot out all distracting thoughts from your mind. Tell yourself that the speaker has something important to say.

2. Concentrate on the speaker. Look him straight in the eye.

3. Let the speaker know you are listening by asking occasional questions.

4. When the circumstances call for it, make notes. I almost always do, and I expect my subordinates to do the same.

5. Listen between the lines. If you're dealing with a diplomat (lucky you!), listen for subtle clues about problems. He may be couching them in the softest possible terms.

Making Notes

Note taking is a valuable tool for effective communication. It is impossible to remember what was said during a business conversation. You will become a more effective manager if you make notes of every meeting you have with your boss and with your subordinates as well. Encourage—or even insist—that those who report to you make notes of the subjects discussed when they get together with you. Notes should serve as a guideline, a direction for the action that each of you has agreed to take. It is even more effective when you compare your notes the next day with the others who attended the meeting to make certain that each of you arrived at the same conclusion.

I get suspicious of any associate who sits in a meeting without pad and pencil in hand. When I question him about the fact that he is not making notes, invariably his answer is, "Oh, I'll remember." He never does. It's virtually impossible, except for a person who has total recall, and I've never met such a person. I can't force anyone to take notes at a meeting, and I try not to be too critical of my associates, but it is difficult for me to respect the business judgment of the person who sits in a meeting without the tools that are necessary to record what is discussed. I regard note taking as essential for an effective manager.

We recently brought a new man into our administrative department. I met with him one day and asked to have some information extracted from our accounting records. I was dissatisfied with the way that overhead was being allocated between our Los Angeles, New York, Washington, and London offices. I asked that an analysis be done that would give me the information I was looking for; my instructions were fairly complex. I was surprised, therefore, to see my new associate sitting in front of my desk, nodding his head to indicate his understanding of what I was saying, but taking no notes.

"Aren't you going to take notes?" I asked.

"No, I never do," he replied, and then mentioned something about writing it all down when he returned to his office.

Far be it from me to contradict a man who has been handling accounting and administrative duties for twenty-five years. Maybe he's one of those rare creatures who listens and then stores everything away in his head. I decided not to force the issue. I would wait and see.

Three days later the report arrived on my desk. It was obvious that many hours had been spent in its preparation. It was neatly typed. I had no complaint about the way it looked. The problem was that the report had no relationship to the information I had asked for. I investigated because I was curious to learn what had happened, and after asking a few questions I discovered the answer. The administrator had turned over my request to the controller, who in turn had verbalized it to a clerk in the accounting department. Here I had discovered a group of professional adults who were still playing the "telephone" game, but who were unaware that they were acting unprofessionally and doing a disservice to themselves and to their company.

A bit frustrated, but not yet in a rage, I called our administrator in to show him the report. It had not been shown to him before for some unknown reason. He didn't know why I was upset, but once he looked at the report he admitted that it was incorrect. He apologized and stated that the errors would be corrected posthaste. He still didn't make a note. He was still convinced that he remembered everything. Two days later the report came back. It still wasn't what I wanted. Now I was completely frustrated. Rules are made to be broken occasionally, and although I believe in following protocol in my office, I decided that this was one of the rare times that breaking a rule was justified.

I called in the clerk from the accounting department. She had been doing all the work, but on the basis of imprecise instructions. Now, without my telling her to do so, she took pad and ballpoint pen in hand and notated exactly the information I wanted. A half hour later the correct report was on my desk.

You must listen to your associates, you must listen to your boss, and equally important, you must write down as a reminder for the next day and days after the basic content and major points of what you have been listening to.

ROGERS' RULES ON NOTE TAKING

1. Take notes when your boss speaks with you. He'll be impressed when you walk into his office with pencil and paper in hand.

2. Take notes when your subordinates speak with you. You'll put them at ease, and they will realize that you value what they have to say.

3. Keep your notes brief. You're making notes as a reminder to yourself of what transpired at a meeting. The notes are for you, not for your colleagues. Later on, you might want to use them as the basis of a memo to your staff.

4. Don't let note taking substitute for listening. If someone is going too fast and you're missing the next point while writing down the last one, don't be afraid to ask him to slow down.

Speaking Plainly and Clearly

I know you think you heard what I said but what you don't understand is that what I said was not what I meant.

Are you guilty? Do people often miss the point you're trying to make? Do they misunderstand or mishear you? "No, not me," I hear all of you saying again. "I have no trouble making myself understood." I have a hunch that your associates might not agree with you. I am regarded as a successful person; I am very conscious of the importance of speaking plainly and clearly. Yet I find that this sensitive subject has always given me a problem. Let me suggest that if it remains a problem for me, you might want to consider that it may also be a problem for you.

Let me give you one example of a situation in which I had to learn the hard way. We had decided to offer Denise, one of our division heads, a new contract. We were gearing up for an aggressive expansion in her area, and I was asked to negotiate a new contract with her.

At our meeting I outlined an offer and spelled out in detail both what we expected from her in the future and what she could expect from us. Denise and I had a provocative, frank discussion, which concluded with her saying that she would think over my offer and get back to me with an answer in a few days. I thought that the meeting had been very productive and forgot about it, confident that I would receive an affirmative answer in the morning.

The following day two of my associates descended on me. "What the hell happened?" they asked in unison. "What did you do to Denise?" I didn't understand what they were saying.

"Do to her?" I responded incredulously. "I didn't 'do' anything to her—except talk straightforwardly about our future plans and offer her a new contract. You make it sound like I called her on the carpet."

"That's exactly what she thinks happened," they responded. Denise had met with them that morning. She was very upset about her meeting with me, but had been good enough at keeping her composure that I hadn't noticed. As I thought back on our meeting, I began to realize what had happened. Although I had made Denise the offer, I had also voiced a series of complaints—minor quibbles, really—about her behavior. Instead of presenting the offer as a major vote of confidence, I had left her feeling that, despite the offer, I would prefer not to have her with our organization.

I was guilty. I became angry—with myself. Whatever criticisms I had about her work most certainly could have and should have waited for another time. Denise had completely misinterpreted what I said to her, but it wasn't her fault, it was mine. It was my responsibility to make certain that she was receiving the message that I was sending out, but she hadn't. I'd blown it. It was a classic case of a failure to communicate.

What to do? There was never a question in my mind. Denise had to be straightened out, reassured that she was a valued member of our team. How to do it? I suggested that Warren Cowan join me in the process. We asked Denise to come in to see us. She arrived in my office very apprehensive, perhaps fearing the worst.

I jumped right in with both left feet. "Denise," I began, "do you remember that last year I wrote a book called *Rogers' Rules for Success?* The subject matter was psychorelations, which I explained was the tool we use to sell ourselves to other people. I got a lot of favorable comment about that book. Many people from all over the country wrote to tell me how much they had been helped in both their personal and professional lives by reading it.

"Well, Denise," I continued, "I'm going to go home tonight and re-read that book. In fact, I'm going to read it half a dozen times, because I really blew it with you. In our meeting I obviously forgot every word I had written in *Rogers' Rules*. I did everything I told my readers not to do. The fact of the matter is that I am very enthusiastic about our future relationship and I apologize for having given you any other impression. I'm sure Warren will be happy to back me up on this."

Warren reiterated our confidence in Denise, and she accepted our contract offer. With my inability to communicate clearly, however, I had made something uncomfortable and difficult that should have been pleasant and easy. When you are trying to make a positive impression, don't mix it with criticism. That was my mistake.

Lawyers and accountants have difficulty communicating with me because I never understand what they are saying. I speak and understand layman's English but I do not understand the jargon of the legal and accounting professions. I have always suspected that most of the clients of members of these professions don't understand what they are talking about but are ashamed to admit it. I have no such shame. I question practically every word or phrase that they utter until I finally understand the content of a document I am asked to sign. They find me a frustrating client. They are frustrating to me too. I wish they would learn to write and to speak plainly and clearly.

A lawyer once sent me a long letter of explanation accompanying papers that required my signature. I returned everything unread with a note that said simply, "Please translate." He was furious, but so was I.

I have always indoctrinated my associates with the rule that they should never leave a situation involving a client until they have a complete understanding of what the client wants. Paul and Samantha asked me just recently to get involved with Steve Martin, one of our clients. It was on a matter that involved Steve's outstanding collection of contemporary art.

Steve and I met early one evening in the bar at the Carlyle Hotel in New York. I ordered a scotch and soda; Steve ordered a Perrier.

"I'm sorry I had to bother you with this silly problem," he said, "but Samantha and Paul insisted that we get together. They just aren't able to understand my attitude about this matter."

"Don't be sorry about anything," I replied. "I've always been a great admirer of yours since those early 'Saturday Night Live' days, and I've seen every one of your films. All the time that you've been a client, we've never met. I'm delighted that contemporary art has finally brought us together. Tell me, what is it that Samantha and Paul don't understand?"

Steve explained that a prestigious magazine, at Samantha's instigation, wanted to do a cover photo layout of him and his collection at his Beverly Hills home, with comments from him on the background and history of the various pieces and his analysis of each work. The two Rogers & Cowan people and the editor of the magazine couldn't understand why he had rejected the idea.

We spent a leisurely hour talking about art, his career, and a new script he was writing. When he left he invited me to drop by and see him and his collection the next time we were both back in Beverly Hills.

The following day I gave my associates a long explanation of the Steve Martin problem, which I will summarize here. Steve was agreeable to doing the layout. He objected strenuously to the magazine's request that he do a commentary on each work of art. He felt that it would be presumptuous for him to place himself in the role of an art critic or writer. He had suggested that the magazine get John Russell of *The New York Times* or William Wilson of the *Los Angeles Times* to do the critique. Paul, Samantha, and the editor did not understand Steve's reasoning. They regarded Steve Martin as an expert on contemporary art, and they consequently could not understand his refusal to write the commentary on his own collection. Steve, with proper humility, realized that although he was an expert in the eyes of his public relations representatives and the magazine editor, he was not an art expert to an art expert.

I then told them the ancient Hollywood story of the writer who left his humble apartment in the Bronx and went to Hollywood to make his fortune. He did, and soon after, he returned to the Bronx to see his mother. His mother looked at him and said, "Son, what kind of a silly cap are you wearing with the gold braid on it?"

"Mama," replied the son, "that's a yachting cap."

"Why are you wearing a yachting cap?" she asked.

"Mama," said the son, "I made so much money writing in Hollywood that I bought a yacht. I'm the captain!"

Mama looked at her son skeptically, shook her head in disbelief, and said, "My darling son, to me you're a captain, to you you're a captain, but tell me, to a captain are you a captain?"

After they finished laughing, Paul and Samantha agreed that they now understood what Steve Martin had been trying to tell them.

ROGERS' RULES FOR SPEAKING PLAINLY AND CLEARLY

1. Think before you speak. The old adage, "Make sure brain is engaged before putting mouth in gear" still rings true.

2. Adjust your speaking pattern to fit your audience. Whatever your profession—medicine, law, public relations—don't use jargon when you talk to laymen. Surely you are clever enough to find a way to use plain English.

3. Don't talk down to people.

4. Speak slowly. Most of us speak too fast.

5. Don't speak *at* someone, speak *with* them. This means *no monologues*.

6. Pause to ask questions, even when you find yourself doing most of the talking (maybe *especially* when you find yourself doing most of the talking). Use questions that require other than a yes-no response. Never ask "Do you understand?" You'll get a no answer only once in the bluest of moons.

7. If you're giving instructions, ask the recipient to repeat in his own words what he understands the assignment to be.

8. Use written communication to back up oral communication. When major topics have been discussed, a memo should be prepared outlining the points made, tasks assigned, schedule, and follow-up responsibilities.

Getting It Down in Black and White

I'm always impressed by someone who's a particularly good writer. At the same time I'm horrified by how poorly most people write—even college-educated people. The problem is usually length. Not being able to write one page, they write five. Most business people, myself included, don't have time to read an inter-office memo that is five pages long. You'll find that people pay far more attention to what you write if you write less of it.

Many people are overly fond of what I call the Paper Trail. They leave memos and correspondence and interim reports and preliminary findings behind them like footprints in wet sand. Enough already! Let me assure you that every executive thinks he has too much reading material piled up on his desk. Some memos are necessary. Others are written just to score points with peers and bosses.

Then there are the people in our office—and in every other office, I assume—who want to make certain that everyone knows what they are doing every moment of the eight-hour day. Copies of every letter and every memo are sent to everyone even remotely connected with the client. I remember a three-line letter that recently went to a client reminding him about an interview that had been set up with a reporter from the *Pasadena*

Star-News. I counted the copy list under my associate's signature. There were seventeen names! Eight went to Rogers & Cowan staff members, nine to people who were associated with the client. I thought of the secretarial time involved and the cost of the stationery, envelopes, postage, and handling in our mail room. I then multiplied that number by two hundred, which I estimated was the number of similar letters and memos that went out of our office every day, multiplied that number by seventeen, and shuddered when I computed the total daily cost.

That day I asked our department heads to speak to their associates and suggest that they send copies to everyone when they wished to announce an impressive article in *Life*, *Time*, *Newsweek*, and similar publications—but not the *Pasadena Star-News*.

Gordon Stulberg, president of Polygram Corporation, told me this amusing anecdote about memos: "A senior executive to whom I would address memoranda would always respond by scribbled notes across the bottom, which I found, at times, to be quite irritating. Rather than chastise him, I decided to fight fire with fire by scribbling *my* responses to letters and other documents that emanated from his office. I'm left-handed, and you can well imagine the problem he had in deciphering a number of them. Eventually, he began to adopt my habit of writing a memorandum where a significant response was required. In turn, I adopted his scribbling type of response when I needed only to make a simple comment."

Stulberg shows excellent judgment in being flexible enough to adopt some of his employees' methods and also in trying to cut down on the volume of paper. What is the middle ground? It's a matter of judgment, but I believe that generally, Less is More.

ROGERS' RULES FOR THE PAPER TRAIL

1. Brevity is the soul of wit. Keep it short and to the point. I call it the Sergeant Friday Approach: "Just the facts, ma'am."

2. Be a soldier in the war against red tape. If a subordinate gives you a long-winded memo, give it back. Tell him (nicely) to take the Sergeant Friday Approach.

3. Don't generate paper needlessly.

4. Edit yourself. Put the main points at the top. Expound upon them (if you really *have* to) further down in the text.

Asking Questions

The smartest people I know are the people who are not afraid to ask intelligent questions. The dumbest people I know are those who are afraid they will look stupid by asking questions. They don't understand that every intelligent boss respects the subordinate who asks questions.

If you are to be an effective manager, you must ask questions of the people who report to you and encourage them to besiege you with questions as well.

This doesn't mean you should become the Grand Inquisitor with your boss. You must be careful not to become too intrusive, because that would hurt your relationship. Here is where your psychorelations skills come into play. Put yourself in the other person's shoes. Will this next question embarrass him? Are you pushing too hard? Is there an indirect way of asking that will produce the same response?

What kind of questions should you ask? Questions related to business performance. Direct, personal questions that intrude on privacy endanger the relationship. Questions such as "Who was that woman I saw you with?" "Did you have three or four martinis at the office party last night?" and "Were you and your wife having an argument when I saw you last night?" are almost guaranteed to put someone on the defensive, which is the exact opposite of what you are trying to achieve.

Let me give an example of how intrusive questions can endanger a relationship. My daughter Marcia Ross called me one day to say, "Daddy, we just returned from New York. We met a fascinating man at a party and we invited him to be your house guest for six weeks!" To say that I was taken aback is the ultimate understatement. A stranger? In my house? For six weeks?

"He'll stay in your guest house. You'll never see him. His name is Mischa. He doesn't speak English too well, and by the way, Daddy. He has a dog."

"Marcia, I'm your father. You can't do this to me. You know how I hate dogs. What kind of dog? Why isn't this guy staying in a hotel?"

"You can't stay in a hotel with a two-hundred-pound German shepherd, Dad. Besides, the fans and papparazzi hound him to death. He has no privacy." At about this point I became apoplectic. "What about my privacy?" I wailed. "Just who the hell is this guy?"

Marcia giggled. "Oh, Dad. Everyone knows who Mischa is. He's Mikhail Baryshnikov, the greatest ballet dancer in the world. He'll be in town making *The Turning Point* with Shirley MacLaine and Anne Bancroft. I already told Mom. She's all excited and she's started to get the guest house ready."

As unhappy as I was, I could see I'd been outmaneuvered. The invitation had been extended; my wife was changing the sheets. And I wasn't about to argue with a two-hundred-pound German shepherd.

I found Mischa sitting by the pool, with dog, when I returned home from work one evening. The two had obviously been swimming. Despite the manner in which I had been roped into this situation, I admired him greatly and was secretly delighted to meet him. I invited him into the den for a drink. Mercifully he left his giant beast outside. "What would you like?" I asked.

"Do you have Stolichnaya?" he asked.

"Of course," I replied. I took out two tumbler glasses, filled them with ice, and poised the bottle over the first glass. "Say when," I said, and began to pour. When he said "when" I handed it to him. He smiled, sipped it tentatively, and sat down. I poured myself a similar drink and sat down facing him.

How someone could convey such power onstage and look like such a boy in person I'll never know. He looked almost fragile, with his blond hair plastered to his head, bare feet placed firmly on the floor. I asked him some gentle questions. How did he like California? Was this his first experience with motion pictures? What dances would he be doing in the movie? He was warm, gracious, and friendly in his answers. Although he kept apologizing for his bad English, I thought he spoke remarkably well for the year or so that he'd been in the States.

It was a pleasant evening. Our nightly chats became a habit. He wanted to know as much about me as I did about him. I always kept my end of the conversation to a minimum, however. One evening my questions became more personal, more intimate. I asked about his life in the Soviet Union, his parents, the rest of his family. He answered my questions guardedly. I felt he was a bit uncomfortable. But I persisted. I finally asked him why he defected.

At the time I failed to notice what in retrospect I now see all too clearly. I had broached a subject Mischa did not want to discuss. My fascination with his past prevented me from seeing him become restless in the chair, looking for a way to change the subject or excuse himself. I don't remember exactly what I said, but his building discomfort erupted. Mischa froze, his pale complexion flushed pink. He stood up. "I don't like this," he said. "You've gotten too personal. I don't want to talk about my personal life." With that he started toward the door.

I tried to apologize, and told him I was sorry I had intruded on his privacy. Although he shrugged it off, saying, "It's nothing, it's nothing," it was never the same after that. Most evenings when I got home he was no longer sitting poolside. If he was, he'd jump up and leave when he saw me. I've not had a really personal conversation with Mikhail Baryshnikov since that day. He continues to be friendly when I see him at dinners, at parties, and backstage at the ballet, but our friendship will never be the same.

I've no one but myself to blame. I was too intrusive, too personal with an intensely sensitive person. Learn your lesson from my mistake: it is important for you to get to know your boss and your subordinates, but you must determine in each case the line between sensitivity and intrusion. Intruding on the intimacies of your associates' personal lives is a mistake, and when you cross that line you are taking the chance that you will ruin your relationship with that person.

ROGERS' RULES FOR ASKING QUESTIONS

1. Begin with the easy ones. If you get monosyllabic responses to "Nice weather we're having" or "How was your day?" a red flag should go up in your brain. And you should close your mouth.

2. Don't pump relentlessly. If you strike a nerve, back off.

3. Give as much as you get. My first mistake with Mischa was probably in not conveying as much about myself as I wanted to know about him.

4. Encourage your subordinates to ask questions about
- procedures to improve their performance;
- items of office etiquette that they are unsure about;
- when it is appropriate to go over your head;
- when they don't know how to handle a problem with a client or customer, with a colleague—or with you.

4

The Power of Positive Criticism

John Robinson, the perennially successful football coach of the University of Southern California and now the Los Angeles Rams, says that he never criticizes his players until they are convinced that he has the utmost confidence in their abilities. Once that has been accomplished, he tells them that they are ninety-nine percent great, so now, "Let's work on the one percent factor that's left."

Robinson demonstrates the revolutionary Rogers motto: criticism should be like a sandwich. If you want to motivate people, slip the criticism in between layers of praise. Many managers give out only the bad news, never thinking to compliment their subordinates for a job well done. How do you offer criticism? How often do you tell people what a good job they're doing? When others criticize you or praise you, do you know how to respond?

Dishing Out Criticism

I noticed Dan walking down the hall, his shoulders slumped, his head hanging low on his chest. "What's wrong?" I asked.

"I just left Alan's office and he read the riot act to me."

"What happened? Why would he do that?" I responded.

"I don't wanna talk about it," he replied. "If Alan thought I came crying to you then I'd really be in the soup."

He shuffled off, obviously dejected, with his hands buried in his pockets. If I had been looking for an unmotivated public relations person, Dan would have been the perfect example.

I walked into Alan's office. "What's wrong with Dan?" I asked. "He looked as though he was wearing sackcloth and ashes and had the weight of the world on his shoulders."

Alan bristled. I watched as he tensed up and asked, "Why do you ask? Did he come crying to you?"

"No," I replied. "I happened to see him walking out of your office and he looked as if he had been hit on the head with a sledgehammer."

Alan told me the whole story—from his point of view. He had raked Dan over the coals for a minor mistake and had left him feeling humiliated. I was anxious to tell Alan that he had acted emotionally and that his unreasonable criticism of his subordinate was inexcusable, but I held my tongue. The timing was not right for me to tell him how badly he had handled this situation. He was upset because he knew that he had treated his employee in an excessive manner, and he was even more upset because he was trying to rationalize and justify his behavior.

When he finished, I just nodded and said, "It's too bad, Alan. Dan's a good man, and we're fortunate to have him." I said nothing more and left the office.

Over the next few months, I had a number of different talks

with Alan about dishing out criticism. I never mentioned the incident with Dan, but I really felt that my soft-sell approach was paying off. I knew it when I ran into Dan leaving Alan's office several months later. This time he was smiling. His head was held high and he was walking with a jaunty gait. "Why are you so perky this morning?" I asked.

"I don't know what's gotten into Alan," Dan replied. "He's a changed man. I screwed up a situation the other day and when he called me into his office this morning I thought I was going to catch hell—again! Instead, he told me what a great job I'd been doing, made a casual remark about my screwup, and then finished off by saying that I was coming up for salary review in a few months and he was going to recommend me for an increase." Dan grinned. "He's not sick, is he?"

"No, he's not sick," I replied with a smile. "Maybe he's just begun to understand how to work with you."

What happened to Alan between my first and second encounters with Dan? I gave him my crash course on the power of positive criticism. He may or may not have known what I was up to. Without making a point of it, during a series of informal meetings, occasional lunches, coffee breaks, and dinners after office hours, I demonstrated the proper way to administer criticism. The basic tenets are simple. The hard part is remembering to use them when it counts.

You should have only one motive in criticizing your subordinates—motivating them to improved performance. How do you accomplish this? Certainly not by telling them that they are incompetent. This will turn them off, which is just what you don't want to do. You want to turn them on—you want to motivate them to do better next time. Give them a Rogers Criticism Sandwich. Start with the premise that there is no such thing as constructive criticism. It may sound constructive to you, but no matter how delicately you put it, he'll regard it as destructive.

Tell him how great he is. Tell him what a fine job he's doing. Tell him that there may have been a better way of handling that particular situation (which you and he both know he messed up), but *allude* to it, don't beat him over the head with a blunt instrument. Finally, wind up by impressing him with your deep appreciation for all his efforts. This is a long, circuitous route to point out his foul-up, but remember—your objective is to motivate him, turn him on, not off, and to get him thinking about how he can avoid making the same mistake next time.

ROGERS' RULES FOR DISHING OUT CRITICISM

1. Keep your objective in mind at all times. Your goal is to motivate people toward higher performance.

2. Sandwich your criticism between two thick layers of praise.

3. Direct your criticism at *what*'s wrong, not *who*'s wrong.

4. Don't tell George that you think his co-worker Harry's work is slipping. Tell Harry. Never criticize a third party to his co-workers.

5. Don't yell. Don't threaten. This results in poorer rather than better performance.

6. End the conversation on an upbeat note. That's the bottom layer of the Rogers Criticism Sandwich. Make sure he leaves your office with a smile on his face.

You Can Dish It Out, But Can You Take It?

Learning how to accept criticism is just as important as learning how to dish it out. Here is a perfect example of the one-

85   210.01.01.10   05/27/90 17.10 5627
B.DALTON BOOKSELLER OKLAHOMA CITY, OK

```
0831769610                        9.98
0790993562                        2.98
0790932903                        2.98
0790993252                        1.98
                  SUBTOTAL       17.92
                  SALES TAX       1.30
                  TOTAL          19.22
6011005764000942 DISCOVER        19.22
```

----------------THANK YOU----------------

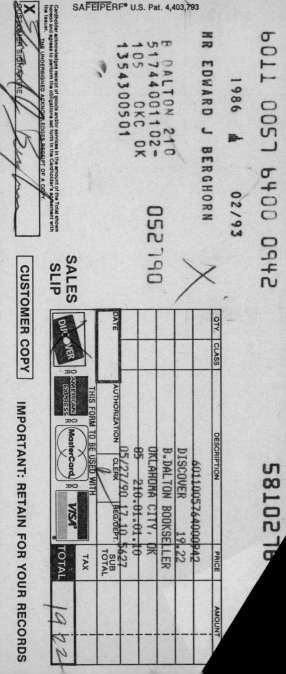

SAFEIPERF® U.S. Pat. 4,403,793

6011 0057 6400 0942

MR EDWARD J BERGHORN
1986 4 02/93

B DALTON 210
5174400102-
105 CKC OK
1354300501

052790

5810278

SALES
SLIP

CUSTOMER COPY

IMPORTANT: RETAIN FOR YOUR RECORDS

QTY.	CLASS	DATE	AUTHORIZATION	DESCRIPTION	PRICE	AMOUNT
				6011005764000942		
				DISCOVER 19.22		
				B. DALTON BOOKSELLER		
				OKLAHOMA CITY, OK		
				85 210-01-01.10		
		05/27/90 17.10.5627				

THIS FORM TO BE USED WITH
CLERK   REG./DEPT.

	SUB TOTAL	
TAX		
TOTAL		

hat solution. You should criticize your employees as you would like and expect your boss to criticize you. You should also react to criticism from your boss exactly as you hope your subordinates will react to criticism from you.

That is the ideal situation, of course, but let's be practical. I am going to assume that your boss is not as intelligent and as subtle in criticizing you as I hope you will be from now on. Let's suppose that no one has told him about the Rogers' Sandwich Theory. You're beginning to feel that he's picking on you. How do you handle it? How do you react? Remember that your reaction will have much to do with how he regards you, both as a person and as a subordinate. If your reaction is resentful, you're going to turn him off. If you can accept his criticism graciously, you will turn him on, and you will have taken one more step in managing your boss.

You must listen carefully without interrupting, even though you believe his criticism is unjustified. In most cases, the reaction that will please him the most is to initially take the blame and apologize. You know that he doesn't like to be contradicted. Does this bother you? It shouldn't and won't if you remember that you're playing a game. After he has made all his points and he knows that in principle you are accepting his criticism, then it's okay to take issue with him, particularly if you feel he has incorrectly stated the facts. You can say, "You're ninety-nine percent right, but there is one point that I would like to clarify. . . ." If he takes issue with you, don't be reluctant to pursue your position. Then back away. You have made your point. You have asserted yourself. You have once more established your self-respect. There is no point in trying to prove him wrong. Don't try to win the game. Just play the game. Tomorrow this situation will be forgotten and you will have another problem to handle.

Forget the question of who is to blame. Work on solving the problem—and quickly. Keep your long-term objective in mind—managing your boss.

ROGERS' RULES FOR ACCEPTING CRITICISM

1. Try to keep your composure and stay in control. The louder he talks, the softer you talk.

2. Don't interrupt. Let him finish before you respond.

3. When you respond, begin by admitting that you're wrong, even if you are not. This throws him off guard. Learn the language of tactical surrender: "I appreciate your taking the time to tell me this"; "I agree. There's no doubt I could have handled the situation better." Then, without contradicting him, tell him your version of the situation. Don't cop a plea. Don't blame anyone else.

4. Ask him how he would have handled the situation under similar circumstances. (You are turning the situation around and asking him to help you solve the problem.)

5. Beware of red flag words that make it sound like you're passing the buck: "No, I didn't." "It's not my fault." "No one told me I was supposed to . . ." "You've got the facts all wrong."

On Praising Your Subordinates

Nothing motivates an employee better than a pat on the back. Whether you stop one of your associates in the hall and tell her how impressed you were with the report she just sent to a client, how well she handled herself at a staff meeting that morning, or how much you admire the dress she is wearing, you are going to leave her with a smile on her face and a confident bounce in her walk. We are all peacocks. You, me, all of us. We like to preen ourselves, we like to be given an opportunity to strut our stuff, we enjoy being stroked and massaged. The more we are massaged, the more motivated we become. Starting with that as a premise, you should find every opportunity to praise the players on your team. Make certain that your praise is truthful. If it is just idle flattery, if they sense that it is just part of a routine you have developed for yourself, it will kick back. "What's gotten into him?" your subordinates will ask. "He's become a con artist."

Edward Carter, chairman emeritus of Carter Hawley Hale Stores, Inc., told me, "I have found that in virtually all cases, employees or associates respond most favorably to appropriate recognition of the job they are doing, and in fact perform better if such recognition is given them. It is even more effective if other, preferably more highly positioned, members of management either express or write notes of appreciation for outstanding work—the effectiveness of people's work, in addition to being influenced by pay, power, and title, can also be significantly affected by appropriate personal or public acknowledgement of their successful accomplishments."

Joan Crawford always knew how to get the most out of me. Whenever I was responsible for an important article about her that appeared in print, I received a phone call from her. "Thank you, darling," would be her opening remark, followed by a minute or two of compliments, concluding with "My love to you, Roz, and the children." I pride myself on giving my clients a one hundred percent effort, but if there is such a thing as a one hundred fifty percent effort, that's what Joan Crawford received from me, because she knew how to motivate me with praise. I represented her for ten years and always had a tendency to devote more time to her than her fee justified, because she unfailingly expressed her appreciation for everything I did.

Praise as a motivator also works in advance. I'll never forget my first meeting with a representative of the Ford Motor Company. I left the executive offices floor at world headquarters in Dearborn, Michigan, with a "high" that no elixir can match. In general, it's the job of a public relations person to sell himself and his organization to the client. At this meeting, for the first and only time in my life, I had a client sell himself to me!

Walter Hayes, Ford's public relations chief in Dearborn at that time, invited me to consult with them on the company's public relations problems. Never before had a prospective client said that he was grateful for my interest.

Did it work? It certainly did! I left that meeting feeling as though a long-forgotten uncle had just left me ten million dollars in his will, and I was ready to devote twenty-four hours of every day to the public relations problems of the Ford Motor Company. Subsequently I've used the approach myself. I tell my associates that I need them more than they need me. Over and over I've seen members of our organization make superhuman efforts because they know someone appreciates it. Praise pays.

ROGERS' RULES FOR PASSING OUT PRAISE

1. Above all, be sincere. If it's just idle flattery, if people believe that it's just "part of your act," it will backfire, to your detriment.

2. If you can, get your boss, or your boss's boss, to give the praise to employees. Soldiers appreciate a medal from the general even more than from the captain. Generals are supposed to give out medals and ribbons; it's one of the pleasures of rank. Besides, most senior executives like to be made aware of who the most promising staff members are.

3. Criticize in private; praise in public. Make sure other staff members are made aware of the outstanding performance of one individual. Applause is a powerful form of praise. It is more important for a person to be applauded in front of his peers than to receive a big bonus that no one knows about.

4. If recognition comes from a source outside the company, make that praise public knowledge. A letter from a client praising a job well done or a civic commendation for public service are important forms of praise, the more so because they come from "impartial sources."

Praising the Boss

It's difficult for you to believe, but your boss could be just as insecure as you are. He may be a tiger in the office, but he might be a pussycat at home because he's scared stiff of his wife. Which means that he's a human being just like you and me, and he likes to be stroked just as much as you do—just as much as your subordinates do. You probably never thought of it before, but I unequivocally recommend that you begin to compliment him on his accomplishments. Never be reluctant to tell him what a good job he is doing. Send him a memo complimenting him on something he did or said. Express your appreciation for the help he gives to you and your team. Give him a compliment, but make certain that it is deserved. Don't give him the opportunity to speculate on whether you are conning him or indulging in idle flattery.

What is to be gained by your aiming some of your praise in his direction? It is one more step in managing your boss. He will become more aware of you, pay more attention to what you have to say, and be more apt to recognize the contribution you are making to the company. When your name comes up for a salary increase or a new contract, your position with him will be stronger than it might otherwise have been.

You can think of a hundred opportunities for patting him on the back, if you put your mind to it. Don't be obvious; don't be cloying; don't be subservient. This is not apple polishing; don't make it look like idle flattery. Just look for opportunities to give him honest praise when you believe he deserves it. It will be another step forward in managing your boss.

How to Accept Praise

Strange as it may seem, many people don't know how to accept praise for a job well done. For some reason they tend to blush, dig their toe into the carpeting, and say, "Ah, shucks, it was nothing" instead of, "Thank you." If you're good at your work, you will, I hope, continue to receive compliments. You should get used to it and know how to deal with it politely and graciously.

I am always impressed when a person thanks me for a compliment. I am particularly impressed when the thanks come in the form of a personal letter. Knowing the favorable impression such a letter makes on me, I have in recent years adopted a policy of thanking strangers for letters they send me. When my first book, *Walking the Tightrope*, was published in 1980, I began to receive "fan mail" from readers who told me that at long last I had explained to them what public relations is. *Rogers' Rules for Success* was published in 1984 and produced twenty times as much mail as *Tightrope* did. I began to lecture at UCLA, USC, NYU, and other colleges and universities throughout the country. I appeared as a guest on television talk shows. Each of these activities generated complimentary letters; each letter received a personal reply from me.

You are probably tempted to ask, "Why bother? What business advantage do you get from all that effort?" The answer is "nothing," which makes the above comments seem to be extraneous in relationship to the purpose of this book. Being gracious to someone who offers you a compliment helps you to establish a habit pattern that is inherent in this book's message. Rogers' Golden Rule: do unto others as you would have them do unto you.

ROGERS' RULES FOR ACCEPTING PRAISE

1. Look the person straight in the eye and say, "Thank you."

2. Don't deny that you did a good job. You're not only contradicting someone who's paying you a compliment, you're also admitting (in a backhanded way) that you weren't doing a good job. Instead, say, "I'm glad you thought it was good. I was pleased with the way it came out."

3. Don't nitpick yourself. Don't spoil the compliment by saying "Yes, but the photos should have been bigger" or "I made an arithmetic error on page 14."

4. Don't be a hog; spread the credit around. O. J. Simpson always acknowledged his offensive line. Be sure to share the spotlight with the people who keep you looking good.

5. Take the time to write a thank-you note.

5

Office Bravery

Too many companies are populated—sometimes even run—by cowards: people who are afraid to admit their mistakes, who hide from problems or refuse to shoulder the responsibilities they are paid to assume, passing the buck for things that go wrong. Cowardice may be a strong word, but that's exactly what it is. You may see cowardice all around you. Cowardice may even be accepted in your company. But that doesn't mean that you have to go along. Wouldn't it be wonderful if you could stand up and be a hero instead of being a coward like all the others? Well, you can. Show a little backbone out there, but do so carefully, graciously. You can begin by getting used to saying three little phrases that are heard all too seldom: "I'm sorry but the answer must be no"; "I don't know"; and "I was wrong."

Saying No

There is a right way and a wrong way to say no, and your skills at giving people a negative response can either win their respect or generate resentment. In promoting a recent book I'd written, I appeared as a guest on a television talk show. The interviewer asked me to give spontaneous quickie observations on a number of Hollywood stars I know. He rattled off the famous names— Paul Newman, Robert Redford, Barbra Streisand. For the most part I was able to give him a rapid-fire response. Sometimes I had to hesitate a moment or two to pinpoint one distinguishing characteristic, but when the interviewer asked, "Cary Grant?" I didn't miss a beat. "He says no better than anyone I've ever known," I replied. "He says no in such a way that you love being rejected."

Just recently the strikingly handsome eighty-two-year-old actor and his lovely wife Barbara approached me at Armand Hammer's eighty-seventh birthday party. Out of the eight hundred guests present, the gracious Mr. Grant made a point of working his way through the crowd to talk with me. With the warming, all-enveloping smile that ingratiated him to film audiences worldwide for so many, many years, he said, "Henry, I'm just devastated that Barbara and I won't be able to attend that dinner party given in your honor next month. We've made plans to go to Wimbledon. If not for that we wouldn't miss it." Jokingly, I replied, "Thanks, Cary. Maybe we can get Wimbledon postponed." He laughed. "You get Wimbledon postponed and I guarantee you we'll be there."

That's what I call a warm, gracious way of saying no. Cary Grant could have ignored my invitation. He could have had his secretary call and say he couldn't make it. He could have sent a note declining the invitation. Instead, on a social evening, surrounded by many hundreds of other guests, he remembered the invitation, which was probably stacked on his desk with a hundred others. He sought me out to explain why he couldn't join me. That's the way to say no.

We can all learn a lesson from Cary Grant. Even though he was declining a social invitation, his technique is a masterful illustration of Rogers' Rules in action. Another person skilled at the art of saying no is television production executive Mark Goodson. As he puts it, "Anyone who survives in show business becomes adjusted to rejection. The odds are that about one idea in a hundred makes it. Nonetheless, even veterans are sensitive to a brusque 'no.' I therefore take great pains to explain why I think any particular suggestion is on the wrong track. I never turn thumbs down on a project without a reasonable explanation. I also offer my *own* suggestions for group discussion and encourage the staff to 'fire away' at *my* ideas. I've tried to show that I can take criticism myself, and, hopefully, this sets an example for others."

One of the hardest nos you will ever experience is turning down a subordinate's request for a raise, be it deserved or undeserved. It is particularly painful for you when because of budget constraints or a salary freeze throughout the company you are forced to reject a request that under ordinary circumstances you would have agreed to. No matter how you handle it, your employee will be devastated by your rejection of his request. You can soften the blow by explaining why, making sure your explanation is clear and logical, and ensuring that he does not think of it as a *personal* rejection.

People who have salary requests often telegraph their intentions. A sensitive boss can sense the impending scene for weeks in advance. Even if you know what's coming and know your answer will be no, permit him to make his pitch. Listen to him. Don't interrupt him. If you cut him off by saying no before he has had an opportunity to speak his piece, you will have a deeply resentful employee on your hands. He had probably been rehearsing his speech for many weeks. This is his big moment. Give him the opportunity to say what takes a lot of courage—on the part of anyone. It takes guts to ask for a raise. Sit quietly and listen; don't just give him a perfunctory hearing. Look him straight in the eye; ask him a question or two when he pauses to take a breath; nod in agreement when he makes a valid point. By doing all this you have told him that you care about him, that you are interested in what he has to say.

Now comes the moment when the going gets tough. Your palms get sweaty; you don't want to hurt him. He hopes you are going to say "Okay, you've made your case. I approve your request. You'll get your raise, effective the first of the month." Unfortunately, you're not going to say that. You're going to turn him down. Let's say the raise is deserved but you can't okay it; last month a salary freeze went into effect. Here are a few approaches that may help you to say no graciously but effectively:

> "I agree with you, Dick, but unfortunately there is a salary freeze on, and there is nothing I can do about it."
>
> "You deserve a raise, but I can't approve it because company policy states that in your job category, I cannot give you a higher salary."
>
> "You're certainly entitled to it, but we work on a budget, and it's not within our budget for this particular time period."

Well, you've done it, you've broken the ice and delivered the bad news. Now you must make sure you have not irreparably damaged your relationship with him. You should immediately let your now unhappy employee know that you're on his team. In effect, you should say, "I can't give you a raise now (much as I would like to), but let's you and I try to figure out when and under what circumstances I *can*." Continue the dialogue. You have said no, but you care about him sufficiently to keep the conversation going. Try to keep it pleasant, even though the moment is difficult for both of you.

How about the person who asks for a raise that you feel is not deserved? This calls for even more tact and diplomacy: you must completely reject someone without offending him. Unless you handle it carefully, your employee could hand in his resignation before the day is over. You might not care, but if it happens, it should happen at your convenience, not his. But let's not look at the bleak picture. Let's look at it constructively and devise a tactic that might motivate your rejected employee. Let me give you an example of how to handle a tough situation like this.

One of our department heads, Joseph, walked into my office one day and asked for a pay increase and a new long-term contract. Joseph's timing was terrible, and he should have known it. He and I had had a number of conversations about the fact that neither he nor his department had shown any growth in recent years. A service business survives on growth. It cannot stand still. Although his department was stagnant, barely holding its own, he had the bad judgment to choose that moment to ask for a raise and a new contract. What to do? I talked to him.

"Joseph," I said, "I find it difficult to understand why you're asking me for a raise at this point in our history together. We've been discussing the shortcomings in the performance of your department for some time now. As you know, I've been a longtime admirer of yours. When you first started with our organization, you set a standard for yourself that I was very proud of. Your department began to grow, and you began to grow, but then something happened. The growth stopped. I don't know why. You and I both know that you and your department are not performing as well today as you were a few years ago. I can't understand why you selected this time to have this particular conversation. You have simply disregarded our previous conversations. You're asking for a raise just because another year has gone by, not because of your recent accomplishments. You won't like to hear this, but I don't feel you deserve an increase. But I'm willing to listen. There are always two sides to a story. Tell me yours."

Joseph and I talked for over an hour, uninterrupted. It could have been an ugly confrontation, but it wasn't. It was a soul-searching conversation conducted by two rational people. When our conversation was over, Joseph, though he was disappointed because I had said no, was more motivated and more challenged than he had been for a long time. He understood and accepted the rejection and knew what he had to do to change rejection into approval. Joseph turned his department around. A year later he got what he had originally asked for—because by then he deserved it.

Of course, Joseph is a particularly rational person, and I was able to reason with him. Your subordinates may not be as rational, and you might not be able to handle the unpleasant experience of turning down an undeserved raise without rancor or anger becoming part of the conversation. If you want the employee to remain with you, it is your responsibility to handle such confrontations with tact, understanding, and time. Don't cut off the conversation after you give him the bad news. Keep the dialogue going. Impress on him that you care.

Cary Grant is not the only person in Hollywood who is skilled at saying no. Before starting work on this book, I wrote letters to a number of executives I know, asking their point of view on some of the subjects I have covered. Some responded immediately, with valuable observations that I have included here. Some ignored my letter, didn't take the time to answer. Still others said no, but how they said it is revealing of their character and their executive ability. Lew Wasserman, chairman of the board of MCA, Inc., wrote:

Dear Henry:

You have my very, very best wishes for the success of the new book you're writing. In fact I'm looking forward to reading it. I'd like to help with your request for illustrations and anecdotes, but I have always made it my policy not to give interviews. If I were to make an exception in this case, I'd have to make others and it would defeat my objective. Sorry.

Best personal regards.

Sincerely,
Lew

Barry Diller, chairman of the board of Twentieth Century Fox Productions, wrote:

Dear Henry:

I have received your letter regarding the book you are writing. Congratulations—you are fast becoming a successful and prolific member of the writing community. You are quite right about delegating authority, but when it comes to this special project, I would not want to delegate in any way—nor would I want to devote less than the proper time to my answers. If it is all right with you, I am going to gently say no. You have caught me at a time when I would not be able to serve you as well as I would want to.

But thank you for flattering me—and the best of luck with the book.

Best regards,
Barry

Letters such as these are examples of how you should say no—with graciousness, kindness, and a sense of caring. Learn a lesson from two of our country's most successful executives.

ROGERS' RULES FOR SAYING NO

1. Be gracious. By saying no, you are disappointing someone, letting them down. Do what you can to cushion the blow.

2. Take your time. Saying no almost always takes longer than saying yes. Don't be abrupt. Don't hurry through it. If necessary postpone the discussion until you can give it the time you should.

3. *Always* explain why. It's easy for bosses to believe that they don't have to justify their actions to subordinates. You don't—*unless* you want to motivate them and keep their loyalty.

4. Offer real alternatives. Don't leave the disappointed person hanging with just a simple "no."

5. Don't lie. Transparently phony excuses don't fool anybody. This doesn't mean you can't put the best face on the truth.

6. Make him feel that you are both on the same team. Talk about "we" more than "you" and "me."

7. Don't make the "no" a one-sided harangue. Have a conversation with him rather than launching into a negative monologue, which shuts down further communication. Get the other person involved. Get his feedback to make sure he understands why you've said no.

8. Say no to everyone the same way—nicely.

Saying No to Your Boss

Saying no to your boss is one of the most challenging tasks you will ever face. If you can manage it without offending him, without incurring his ill will, you will have proven yourself not only the bravest but the most tactful of all creatures.

Saying no to your boss on a major issue often involves a matter of principle, and you should make your own decisions based on your own set of principles. This is a case where I cannot advise you, where you must weigh the pros and cons and finally make up your own mind as to your proper course of action. If you need advice, talk things over with your spouse, or your best friend.

Here are some cases where you might be inclined to say no to your boss:

> If you are asked to double your workload or responsibility (or both) without added compensation.
> If you are asked to do something you feel is illegal, unethical, or in direct conflict with written company policy.
> If you are asked to move from Los Angeles to Fargo, North Dakota.

These kinds of issues get thornier as you move up the executive ladder, and even though I can't tell you whether to say yes or no, I can recommend an approach that might help you attain your objective—to say no without offending your boss.

Let's take the move from Los Angeles to Fargo as an example. You can't tell him that you don't want to move because you don't like the climate. That answer, though understandable, is unacceptable from a company point of view. It's selfish. It might even be construed as disloyal. "How could you possibly put your own comfort and well-being above the needs of the company?" your boss may well ask. No one said bosses are always fair and reasonable. In the meantime, how do you get out of this dilemma? Let me talk you through a hypothetical meeting you might have with your boss if he asked you to move to the Fargo office.

Begin with the argument that will carry the most weight—that the move will be bad for the company's bottom line. "I've thought about it," you can say, "and in my opinion such a move would be a big mistake for the company. Let me explain," you continue. "I would have to go through all the agonies of moving my wife and kids, with each of them yelling and kicking all the way from here to North Dakota. Once we got there, they would stay on my back twenty-four hours a day. I would be aggravated beyond endurance, and as a result, my performance level would drop fifty percent—or more. I would be doing a lousy job, and that would be counterproductive for all of us. I wouldn't mind moving to Fargo (*this is a little white lie, but in this instance it's harmless enough*), but I just know that our profits would suffer if I did.

You're off to a good start. You've immediately moved the discussion out of the "I don't want to" arena into the "It's bad for our business" arena. This gets the boss convinced that you are interested in what is good for the business, but you've left him with an unsolved problem. Now offer him an alternative.

"Here's another thought," you continue. "Maybe *we*" (*excellent choice of pronouns! By using "we" you have allied yourself with the boss and you are helping to solve his problem*) "can look for someone who is already based in Fargo. If you would like, I'd be glad to go up there for a day or two and look around. I'll bring back a list of candidates with their résumés. Then you might want to meet with a few of those who seem to have the best potential. Hiring someone who already knows the territory could be a better solution to the problem."

Skillfully done! You're temporarily off the hook and you've given the boss at least one alternative to sending you to Fargo. By the way you've handled it, he can't berate you for saying no because you have told him that it would adversely affect the profits of the company, and you gave him what might be a better solution to his problem. He might not be ecstatically happy because you didn't immediately take the next plane to Fargo, but he also couldn't possibly be angry with you.

ROGERS' RULES FOR SAYING NO TO THE BOSS

1. Don't give him an immediate answer. If it's a big request, call for "time out" and ask for time to think it over.

2. Keep an open mind and actually think it through. Discuss it with someone you trust.

3. Develop a game plan for handling the forthcoming confrontation, keeping tact and gentility uppermost in your mind. Consider the various responses your boss might give you and decide in advance how you will answer each of his arguments.

4. Give him logical business arguments, even if your basic reason is personal.

5. Put yourself in *his* shoes. Give him alternative solutions. Assure him that you are on his team and that you want to help.

I Don't Know

Do you want to impress your boss? Remember that to impress him is to manage him. Do you want him to respect you just a bit more than he does at this moment? Walk into his office and say, "Boss, I need your help. I'm faced with a tough problem, and I just don't know how to handle it."

Have I shocked you? Have I suggested something that you would never dream of doing? It is contrary to what you have always considered "normal" behavior? If so, don't be embarrassed, because you're like most people. Most people will not admit to their bosses that there is anything they don't know, that there is any problem they can't solve, that there is any task that they cannot or will not undertake. Do you really believe that your boss believes that you know *everything?* He's more intelligent than that.

If you regard yourself as secure and mature, you should have no qualms about saying "I don't know." This is particularly true if it involves a subject that is outside the realm of knowledge you are expected to have in your present job. You know your boss is looking for the truth. You also know that he probably enjoys the ego trip of helping one of his staff to solve a problem, to show him how something should be done, or to answer an unanswered question. He can't do any of those things unless you have the guts to walk into his office and say, "I don't know."

Angela asked to see me one day, looking depressed and frightened. I was not accustomed to seeing her like this. She is one of our best account executives and is responsible for supervising the work we do for six very important clients in the entertainment world.

"Angela, what's wrong?" I asked. She was on the verge of tears.

"I hate to bother you with this. It's so stupid. I have a problem with Jack and I just don't know how to handle it. I don't want to blow it. I'm coming to you because I'm stuck and you're the only person who can help me. Do you mind?"

Of course I didn't mind. No intelligent boss does. I told her to stop worrying about bothering me—that's my job. That's what I get paid for—to help solve problems. She filled in the details and then looked at me expectantly. Angela was on the edge of her seat, waiting for the wise old sage to solve her problem. I sat there for a moment and said nothing. The reason I said nothing was simple. I didn't have the answer. "Angela," I began, "we certainly have a tough problem. I can understand why you came to see me. I'd like to ask Warren for his opinion." I asked my partner of thirty-five years, Warren Cowan, to join us in my ofice, and I posed the problem to him. He thought about it for a few minutes. He finally said the magic words that Angela will never forget. "I don't know," he said, and then excused himself because he had left a meeting in his own office in response to my request for a few minutes of his time.

I turned to Angela and said to her directly and forcefully, "What just happened should be one of the most important lessons you ever learn at this company. Warren and I have been in business for thirty-five years. We've had as much experience and probably know as much about public relations as any two people in the United States. Yet we don't have a ready answer for you. You were reluctant, almost ashamed, to admit to me that there was a problem you couldn't solve. You were afraid to say, 'I don't know.' Don't ever hesitate to say it to yourself, to me, or to anyone else. If your two bosses don't know, why should you assume that we expect you to know everything about everything? No one does."

What happened to Angela's problem? I called a meeting right after lunch. Four of us worked on it for half an hour. We finally arrived at a consensus for an approach to the problem. Angela submitted it to the client and he was pleased. He accepted our plan. Since that time Angela drops in to see me a few times a month with a smile on her face and a problem that she doesn't know how to handle. And I think more—not less—of her for it.

Robert Wagner, star of the TV series "Hart to Hart," came in to see me one day. He wanted some advice. He had just come from London, where he had met with the consortium that was attempting to raise the *Titanic* from the icy depths of the North Sea. He had been given the rights to produce a documentary film on the formidable task of bringing the once-great ocean liner to the surface. As he described it to me it was one of the most exciting projects I had ever heard about. I told him so, and then asked him how I could be helpful.

"I know that you represent a number of large corporations, and

I thought you might know of a company that might be interested in investing in this project."

"How much do you think it will take?" I asked.

"We haven't determined a budget as yet, but I would think it would be in excess of a million dollars."

"If you'd like an answer from me right now, I'll tell you that I don't know." I smiled at him. "I must confess, R.J., I haven't had much experience in helping to finance a documentary film on the raising of the *Titanic*. Give me a few days to think it over."

He smiled in agreement. "Think about it and let me know if you have any ideas," he said. We shook hands and he left my office.

Two days later I telephoned him. "I've thought of two companies that we represent, both of which might be possibilities because they pride themselves on their high-tech capabilities. I'm referring to Ford Motor Company and Texas Instruments. When you're ready with your project, I'd be glad to set up appointments for you to meet with the right people."

R.J. thanked me for my interest. The point of the story is that I was not reluctant to say "I don't know" at the moment the question was asked of me. I was not in a position to give him an immediate answer, but in a few days I was able to give him the information he wanted.

(As of this writing, the fate of the *Titanic* still has not been resolved.)

ROGERS' RULES FOR I DON'T KNOW

1. Save the tough ones for the boss. You don't help yourself by asking for his help on a routine matter.

2. Just as you would never say no without an explanation,

never leave someone hanging with a plain "I don't know." Always provide a plan of action, including a date or time when you think you might have the answer.

3. Problem solving can be a good way to build teamwork. Don't just take your difficulties to the boss, take them to your associates as well. They'll probably have some interesting suggestions, and won't you be flattered when they return the favor?

I Was Wrong

There are few things in life we can be really sure of, so it's puzzling to me why we're all reluctant to ever admit that we're wrong. You may be right about a given situation, but if you admit that there is a possibility that you're wrong, you will begin to understand that polarized arguments are counterproductive and time wasting. Think about it. When you back down to your boss or one of your subordinates and say, "Okay. I might be wrong. Let's do it your way," you haven't lost a thing. In fact, you've won. Why? If you *were* wrong, you will be thought of as an intelligent, fair, and rational person who knew when to back away. If you are finally proven right, you're still a hero. You were big enough to let someone try another approach. Once you are proven right, you are in a stronger position than you were before with your boss and with your employees as well.

Think about the people you know who cling to their position in spite of all arguments to the contrary. Think about the names we call them: bullheaded, pigheaded, obstinate, headstrong. Not exactly complimentary. It's the brave person, not the coward, who calls a halt to an office altercation by saying, "Okay, I admit it. I was wrong." Employees become motivated when they become convinced that their input is valuable. Employees become innovative in a climate where it's okay to try new things that don't always work out. Permit them to make some decisions and find their own way of doing things. Be receptive to their suggestions; adopt some of the policies they propose.

What do you do with a tyrant boss who insists that everything be done his way and only his way? If you are a forthright individual with strong principles about right and wrong, you may face a serious problem with an autocratic boss. Nevertheless, I suggest that at some point not far into the disagreement you should back down. You will have lost the battle but won the war. Your long-term relationship is far more important than whether you win or lose this particular altercation.

I'm not recommending abject capitulation, although there are surely some despots who will accept nothing less. There's an old joke that's only halfway funny about the boss who tells an underling, "If you're right one more time today, you're fired!" There is a danger with some bosses in proving yourself right—you may find yourself right out on the street.

ROGERS' RULES FOR SURRENDER

1. Do get your point or points across before backing down. Express your point of view.

2. If you give in on an issue and it later turns out you were right, avoid the temptation to say "I told you so." Hindsight is always 20/20, and no one likes postmortem finger pointing.

3. If you're worried that you might take the rap for someone else's bad judgment, the time to make that clear is before the fact, not after it. If you've just given in with many reservations to your boss or to another associate, write a memo to the parties involved stating the facts, and keep a copy in your files. It will take you off the hook if there are repercussions later.

4. Take a mature attitude toward being wrong. Being right is

definitely better than being wrong, but accept the fact that nobody is right all the time.

5. Learn the language of graceful surrender:

"I don't agree, but one person has to make the final decision. You're the boss and I respect your opinion."

"We've been arguing back and forth and now I'm ready to back down. I see your point of view and admit that your arguments are stronger than mine."

"I'm the boss but that doesn't mean I'm always right. You're the one who's going to have to live with this decision and I'm willing to let you make it."

6

Timing Is Everything

Timing is everything when it comes to motivating your employees and managing your boss. It becomes important in practically every situation, every problem that faces you every business day. When do you ask your boss for a raise? When do you ask to have a meeting with him? Is there ever a good time for a confrontation? When do you give your subordinates a pep talk? When do you lower the boom and when do you raise it? As a middle manager, you must handle each of these questions with timing uppermost in your mind. Why? Because with proper timing, you will attain your objective, but with bad timing you probably won't. You won't get the raise you have been anticipating for so long; your staff meeting will accomplish nothing and your meeting with your boss will turn into a fiasco.

Time for Your Subordinates

In addition to all your other time-consuming activities as a middle manager, you must take the time to supervise and work with your subordinates. Your big problem is to determine how to find the time to get it all done. You had a mountain of work to do before you moved up to your present managerial position. In your new capacity, your biggest problem is to work out the transition into your new position and, simultaneously, to help your subordinates in the transition of their work efforts so that they can readily take over your former responsibilities.

You may have fallen into the same trap that besets many of your peers during the learning process of becoming an efficient manager. Prior to taking on your new assignment, you devoted forty hours a week to specific job responsibilities. While you are taking on the responsibilities of management time required by your new job, you must immediately turn over at least seventy percent of the time you spent at your former job to your subordinates. (I say seventy percent because they cannot immediately take on all of your previous responsibilities.) This is an important turning point in your career. You must effect a two-way work transition—yours and your subordinates, you must take on the new job and at the same time make certain that your old job is being handled properly. If you don't do it immediately, you will soon find yourself drowning in a sea of detail that will prevent you from properly fulfilling the responsibility that you are now being paid for.

We had three months of discussion at one time in our business about moving David into a top management position as a department head. "He can't do it," said some of the skeptics. "He's too busy handling the clients who are now his responsibility."

"He can do it," said some of the more progressive members of our management team. "Let's help him to develop a competent staff of subordinates who will report to him, and they will take on the day-to-day chores of working on the clients."

"It won't work," complained the skeptics. "David won't let go. He doesn't know how to effect a transition. He won't let anyone near his clients, because he refuses to admit that anyone else can do the job as well as he does it."

The progressives had a conclusive answer to that argument. "He won't turn his clients over to anyone else because he has no one else to turn them over to. He has executive ability, but he has been acting only as an account executive. Give him some people to supervise and then we'll work with him to show him how to get other people to take over his present responsibilities." With that, the progressives won the day. David is now running his own department, and very efficiently, too.

Steve is one of our better supervisors, but it took him a long time to make the adjustment from being an account executive, who only had to report upward, to being an account supervisor, who reports upward to a vice president and also has a number of account executives reporting upward to him. He had had a difficult time wearing only one hat. Every time he now looked at himself in the mirror he saw two hats on the top of his head.

One day I asked him how he made the transition. This was his reply. "You tried to help me," he said, "but I soon realized that it was something I had to learn myself. When I first started, I really went out of my mind. I know that you have always advocated the open-door policy. It works for you, but I had trouble with it.

"Every time I started to do something, my intercom would buzz or one of my subordinates would walk into my office with a problem. I was like a daddy," he continued. "One of my children would run into my office crying, 'Fix my toy.' Usually the problem was already solved, but emotionally the associate needed my approval."

"What finally happened?" I asked. "You must have licked it somehow."

"I knew that I had to spend time with my associates. They needed indoctrination. But I was spending the wrong kind of time with them. I was in effect doing their job for them instead of showing them how to do it. I was making the mistake of telling them the solution to the problem, but I never told them how I'd arrived at the solution so they could solve it themselves the next time. I'd go home frantic every night, feeling that I'd left everything in a state of chaos, because I knew I was making no progress in getting us both to make the transition.

"I finally figured out," Steve said proudly, "that I was in a mess of my own making. I was spending too much time doing other people's jobs instead of explaining to them what had to be done and how to do it. When I stopped fixing toys and began handing out screwdrivers with a set of instructions, my work became a lot easier."

Janet is another of my associates who has done a remarkable job making the adjustment from subordinate to manager. She started as a secretary. Janet was bright, ambitious, eager to learn—and she made it clear to everyone that she fully expected to climb up through the corporate structure to an important position as one of our top public relations executives. We were having lunch one day, talking about a number of our clients, when I suddenly changed the subject of our conversation.

"Incidentally," I said, "you never really told me how you managed to move up from secretary to vice-president. It's a remarkable success story and I'm curious as to how you did it."

Janet laughed. "I'm glad you asked. No one ever asked me before, and I must confess that I've been wanting to tell someone the story. I'm glad it's you. First, I looked around and noticed that most people are not ambitious. If they got to be account executives, they seemed to be content to remain in that capacity. I was always ambitious, and decided that if I really worked at learning this business, there was very little competition. I was puzzled because it appeared to me that no one else was interested in learning. I learned this business by educating myself. I took extension courses at UCLA and USC. I attended seminars. I joined our public relations trade associations, and I regularly read every trade paper that is associated with our business. If I had done nothing else, I would have automatically moved ahead of my associates here in the company, but once I got to my first position of authority, I had to figure out what I had to do to move up the next step. I came to a decision at that time, and if there is one determining factor in the success I have had thus far, I believe it was my decision about the importance of prioritizing my time and then my determination to learn how to do it.

"Most people get stuck at one point in their careers because of their inability to delegate responsibility. They are unwilling to delegate authority because they don't take the time that's required to pass on their own fund of knowledge to someone else. I've heard it said a hundred times by some of my associates: "It will take me more time to explain it to him than it will for me to do it myself."

"The first thing I learned was to teach the people who worked for me what I had been doing in my previous position. It was time consuming at first, and I had endless meetings, but the time finally came when those people learned how to perform those chores, leaving me free to take on my new responsibilities as vice-president."

"You make it sound simple," I said, "but there must be more to it than that."

"There are a hundred nuances," Janet continued, "and they all involve prioritizing of time. You know the old cliché about how you can lead a horse to water but you can't make him drink. There is an analogy in management. I found that it's easy to tell people what to do. It also isn't too difficult to get them to do it. The problem, the one that is the real time killer, is to get through to them *why* they are doing what they are doing, what they are accomplishing and why it is important. It's too easy for people to do things by rote. You might as well get a robot. I devoted an enormous amount of time at the beginning explaining to the people who report to me not only what they were supposed to do, and in some cases how to do it, but more important, why they are doing it. Once I got through that, I was able to pass on to them everything I had been doing when I was in their position. Then I had the time to think about my own job."

"Good for you," I said, "I'm very proud of you. I wish we had more people who were as ambitious and as intelligent as you are. Where do you go from here at Rogers and Cowan?"

She laughed again. "Do you really want to know?" she asked.

"I certainly do," was my reply.

"I've got my eye on your seat. Do you mind?"

It was my turn to laugh, "I don't mind at all. Someone's going to get it one day. It might as well be you."

ROGERS' RULES FOR GIVING TIME TO YOUR SUBORDINATES

1. As a middle manager you have two distinct demands on your time. First, the time to handle your own responsibilities. Second, the time to help your subordinates handle theirs.

2. Your subordinates require your personal attention as individuals. Staff meetings have a function, but they are no substitute for one-on-one interaction.

3. Don't resent the time you give them. Remember that they can make you look good—or lousy.

4. Don't do their jobs for them. Explain to them how to do it and why they are doing it.

5. Seek them out. Don't wait for them to ask for a meeting with you.

6. In order to give them sufficient time, you may have to schedule meetings before or after regular office hours. A 7:30 or 8:00 A.M. coffee date is effective for many middle managers. Donald Petersen, chairman of Ford Motor Company, has a weekly 7:00 A.M. meeting with his associates.

7. If you face the predicament of giving time to your subordinates or having time to work on one of your own projects, give preference to the subordinates. As a member of management you cannot be a clock watcher. You must expect to work longer than the normal forty-hour week.

Time for Your Boss

Managing your boss in relationship to his time and yours is not an easy task, but it can be done if a few adjustments are made by each of you. Timing is everything when it comes to handling your boss. You must sense his moods, his workload, his schedule, his likes, and his dislikes and adjust your own behavior accordingly. Do you want to meet with your boss? How important is it? Is it important to you, important to him, or important to the company? Is it something that is better discussed out of the office rather than in the midst of a busy day? Do you want something from him, or are you going to present him with a problem, or are you asking his advice?

Once you answer these questions, it will be helpful to talk with his secretary. What is his mood today? Was he grouchy or unpleasant when he walked in this morning? How is his day shaping up? Does he have some free time at any particular hour? Determine how much time you'll need. If circumstances aren't right for a meeting, try to postpone it for another day.

If there is an emergency and you must see him immediately, make him aware that you know that your timing is not good and that you will get out of his hair as quickly as possible. Your boss is the prime source of your priorities. Don't let this rankle you— that is the price you must pay to be involved in a hierarchy. That's just the way it is, and you must accept it.

As you look at your organization, you can readily see that your boss faces the same problem with his boss. Someone above him on the organization chart is setting his priorities for him. If you are fortunate enough to have an understanding boss, you will find that if you are both flexible, priorities can be meshed so that time problems related to priorities can be overcome.

If you and your boss disagree as to what your priorities should be, you are obligated to try to persuade him to come around to your way of thinking. If you fail, his priorities must become your own. Someone must make the final decision, and in this case, he's the one.

I have strong feelings about employees who want to take up my time, and they are probably the reverse of what you would expect. I have much greater respect for the person who seeks me out than the one who doesn't. The person who wants to meet with me *cares*. He is more than interested, he is devoted. He is ambitious. He is aggressive. He wants to move ahead. He wants to learn. He knows that because of my long experience as a successful entrepreneur, he can learn something from me. I can give him an insight into a problem. I can advise him on how to best handle a sticky situation. For the good of our business, I always make time to meet with any one of my associates who asks for an appointment.

In contrast, I have less respect for the person who makes no effort to establish a relationship with me. Over the years, curious about why certain of my associates don't take advantage of my experience, I have asked questions. The answers go something like the following:

- "I don't want to bother him." (He doesn't understand that the boss wants to be bothered.)
- "I don't want to take up his time." (An effective executive always makes time for his employees.)
- "I want to leave well enough alone." (He's afraid that his boss will find out what he isn't doing.)
- "I'm afraid he'll ask me questions I can't answer." (He's reluctant to admit what he doesn't know.)
- "My problems are too small for him to bother about." (Small problems grow into big problems and bosses know that.)

The responses, to me, show a lack of perception and understanding of the help that is available to one if he wishes to take advantage of it. I believe that most executives would agree with me.

ROGERS' RULES FOR DETERMINING TIME FOR YOUR BOSS

1. Early morning meetings are more productive than those that are held in the mid- or late afternoon. Irritability, impatience, and fatigue increase as the day wears on.

2. If your meeting is not going well because you sense that the boss is rushed, in a bad mood, or is not responding to you, try to break it up. "Let's discuss this at another time," you might suggest. If he agrees, run like hell to the nearest exit.

3. If you wish to see him on the spur of the moment, don't just barge in. Buzz him on the intercom or call his secretary. Make sure if you do so that whatever you have to say is important and demands his immediate attention.

TIMING IS EVERYTHING

Every office is different, and the best advice about timing is to develop good "seat-of-the-pants" judgment about when the time is right and when it is not. You can get some good clues by observation. Watch how other people in the office interact with the boss, paying particular attention to those with the greatest office longevity. Anyone who has been around for three years or more has learned the particular timing that achieves the best results with a particular boss.

Your own common sense will nevertheless always be your best guide. There are, however, a few generalized rules that seem to apply in most organizations I've observed.

ROGERS' RULES FOR TIMING

1. Don't pounce on someone just as he's reaching his desk in the morning. Even something that has to be dealt with right away can wait until I get my coat off, put down my briefcase, say "good morning" to my secretary, and take a sip of coffee.

2. Conversely, don't try to discuss anything with someone who's halfway out the door. "Can I catch you before you leave?" is bad because mentally the person has already left.

3. When you have something troublesome to discuss, if possible don't bring it up first thing Monday morning. No one likes to get hit with a ton of bricks at the top of the week.

4. When you see someone gobbling Tylenol or Bromo-Seltzer, steer clear. Don't expect sweetness and light—or brilliant insight—from someone who has a headache, the flu, or indigestion.

5. During the holiday season from Thanksgiving through New Year's, many people take time off and almost all offices are less than fully staffed. Meeting deadlines is harder, so the holidays are a perfect timing opportunity to prove yourself a hero and pitch in where needed.

7

Hiring, Firing, and Quitting

You will be evaluated many times in your career on the basis of the people you hire and the people you fire, on your behavior when you are hired, quit, or are fired, and the reasons why your subordinates quit your employ. How you handle these office transitions, both your own and others', is a fundamental management skill. Every middle manager must include these items in his areas of responsibility and your career is influenced by the ease and grace (or lack thereof) with which you handle them. You probably don't give much thought to your own behavior when these situations are forced on you, but remember that someone higher up in your organization takes your abilities in hiring, firing, and quitting into consideration when you're being evaluated for a move up the corporate ladder.

135

Being the New Guy in Town

This is your first day on the job. You're the new guy in town, the new middle manager. Let me help guide your behavior so that you get a good start.

Your first move: see your immediate superior. Tell him that you are glad to be with the firm and pleased to be reporting to him. You probably have numerous questions about what is expected of you. Some of these responsibilities were spelled out for you during the job interviews you went through before you were hired, but I'm sure you have a written or mental agenda of many items that are still unclear. Ask him if he has time to see you now. If he doesn't, pin him down for another appointment. It is essential that you see him very quickly, for it will be impossible for you to properly fulfill your responsibilities unless and until you know what is expected of you. Your first task is now completed—you've seen the boss.

Now comes your next move. Introduce yourself to each of the people who report to you. You are probably thinking that it's their job to make a favorable impression on you. Forget it. *You* have to make a favorable impression on *them*. Why? Because they are going to make you look good or bad. Your performance on the job will be directly related to their performance. Remember that you need them as much as they need you—maybe more.

Want to make a good first impression? Go to see them in their offices. Don't ask them to come to see you. They will all be talking about you before the morning is over, saying, "What a swell guy, no fancy airs about him. I'm going to like working with him."

Your conversations with them should be short, warm, and pleasant. You're delighted to be working with them. You need them on your team. You need their cooperation. You will need their help and you will be asking them lots of questions. You have an open-door policy. Each one of them should feel free to come in and see you at any time. With this kind of approach, you're off to a good start.

If you're new in your job, you must make it clear to your subordinates right from the start that things are going to be different for them. They've been working for someone who had his own style, his own guidelines, his own set of expectations for the people who reported to him. Explain to them that you are a different person with a different style, that you realize it will take some time for you both to become accustomed to each other, but they should know that they are all playing in a different ball game with a different captain.

You might find some recalcitrants, some rebels who will object to their having to change their work style and work habits just because a new captain has arrived on the scene. You will have to deal with each one of them on an individual basis. Most of them will come to accept the new order, but if there are some who continue to rebel, you might be forced to get them off your team.

The "new guy in town" is always considered suspect by his subordinates and his peers, and sometimes with good reason. If he has an ego problem, which so many people have, he will have decided in advance that everything the previous manager did was wrong. He will tear everything apart and start all over again. Sadly, he will discover after it is too late, that what was already in place before he arrived was probably better than what he has installed. It is no wonder, then, that the "new guy in town" is suspect.

I often see examples of such behavior in the Hollywood film studios. A new production head is brought in to make the company more profitable. Although his predecessor, who couldn't have been a complete idiot, invested many millions of dollars in literary properties, which were in the process of being developed into screenplays for hoped-for future film productions, the new guy, usually without even considering any of the material, tosses it all onto the junk heap. This is usually Hollywood S.O.P. (Standard Operating Procedure), for two reasons. First, his ego will not permit him to consider that these properties have any redeeming qualities if they were prepared by the person he replaced. Second, if he were to break tradition and produce one of these properties, and if it turned out to be a hit, then he would consider himself to be in real trouble. He would receive no credit from the industry or his peers because the film was originated by someone else. He would also have sleepless nights because he would be convinced that the big boss was having second thoughts about why he had discharged his predecessor.

Incongruous as this S.O.P. and thinking appear to the outsider, it is not indigenous to Hollywood. Ego is a major factor in the American business community, and you should not be surprised when you find it responsible for troubles in your own company.

There is also the positive ego, which has a positive effect. The intelligent executive has an uplifting influence from the moment he arrives and is sufficiently self-confident that he does not feel compelled to rock the boat when he comes on board. His first move is to do a careful analysis of his department, his people, and the projects that are in the development stages. He discards nothing until he is certain that what he has to offer is better than what is now in place. The suspicion that greeted him as he came aboard is soon dissolved, and the morale of his department is enhanced as he moves slowly but firmly in a positive direction.

ROGERS' RULES FOR THE NEW GUY IN TOWN

1. Consider yourself on probation for at least the first six months. This means you should try to be your very best, most charming and industrious self at all times.

2. Set yourself apart from the person you are replacing, no matter how popular he or she was or what the conditions were of his or her departure. If everyone expects you to do things "just like Steve," you'll be playing a comparison game that you'll never win.

3. If you arrive at a volatile time in the department, your first obligation is to "put the troops at ease." Make it clear to your subordinates that no changes will be made until you've spoken with everyone and gathered all the facts.

4. Now, perhaps more than at any other time, it is your job to make the first move in forming new relationships. Don't forget the Power of Lunch as a strategy to build bridges to your subordinates and your boss.

5. Expect the unexpected. Realize that Murphy's Law works everywhere—and continuously. Still, be optimistic and don't permit your subordinates to even suspect that there is a note of pessimism or skepticism in your attitude.

Hiring Your First Employee

I'll confess to you that I have probably made at least as many mistakes in hiring people as most business executives. I consider myself a public relations expert, even a people relations expert, but not a personnel expert. As hard as I try to be objective and impersonal, I occasionally succumb to my emotional instincts. If I am immediately impressed with someone's personality or looks rather than his abilities and qualifications, that person has the inside track with me, at times even in the face of all logic to the contrary.

This may sound amateurish. It is, but every person, no matter how successful he may be, has his weak points, and hiring is one of mine. I sometimes tend to overlook the traits that can be more important than looks or personality. Is the candidate motivated? Why is he out of a job at this moment? How many different jobs has he had in the past ten years? There are a hundred questions I should be asking, but I avoid asking them. Why? Because I'm afraid I'm going to get the wrong answers, answers that will turn me toward someone else—but I don't want someone else. I want this person. My mind is made up. I like him. I hire him and soon I am sorry.

For a time I overcompensated by looking for unattractive people with little personality. Some time ago in our New York office, my associates had interviewed a number of prospects for a corporate public relations position. A prerequisite was that the candidate have strong New York media contacts. The choice had been narrowed to two, at which time I was asked to sit in on the final selection. I found myself confronting one finalist, an unattractive gentleman. Aware of my own unsuccessful track record of leaning toward attractive men and women, I quickly decided not to hold this against him. His qualifications appeared to be in order; his references were impressive. He seemed right for the job. In retrospect, because I had become defensive about leaning toward attractive people, I overreacted, allowing his physical bearing to push me in his direction. We hired him and then I was sorry—again.

It took us three months to be sure we had made another mistake, but it took us another three months to face up to the agonizing task of discharging him. We finally did. Shortly after he departed our premises, I was talking to a San Francisco-based psychologist who had had contact with our ex-employee when he was still in our employ.

"I talked to him for five minutes," said the psychologist, "and I knew right then that he wouldn't be with your firm for long. I found him to be a completely negative person. He didn't like his job. He didn't like the public relations business, and most important, he didn't like himself."

I was impressed, dumbfounded, and angry with myself. I had talked to him for an hour and had seen none of the negative traits that my psychologist friend had observed.

"That's because we were looking at him from two different points of view," he explained. "You were looking for Mr. Good New York Media Contacts. I was looking for Mr. Human Being. I was looking at a person, his motivations, his interests, his personality. You were looking for almost anyone you thought could solve your problem for you. If I had been interviewing him on your behalf, I would have asked him a hundred personal questions before I ever arrived at his professional qualifications."

The psychologist was right. I had broken all my own rules. I had ignored the most subjective but most important attributes of the applicant, his skills at psychorelations—how this person related to people, how people related to him, how he would fit in with the rest of our staff. Most important of all, I had ignored his lack of motivation. In fact, I had never even probed the subject, which should have been the number-one qualification to look for.

I learned an important lesson through this experience. I finally admitted to myself that I was not qualified to hire people. As an owner of my own company, I am entitled to the privilege of avoiding such tasks, but as a middle manager you will not be given the same opportunity. I look for the best qualities in people and don't probe deeply enough to find their worst qualities because I have already decided to hire the attractive young person who is sitting before me. I convince myself that the person is exactly who Rogers & Cowan is looking for and I don't pursue difficult questions that might lead me to discover that I'm wrong.

ROGERS' RULES FOR HIRING

1. An interview is a dialogue, not a monologue. Most interviewers talk too much. It is your job to get the prospective employee to talk, not to get him to nod his head.

2. Put the candidate at ease. Make him feel comfortable. Don't use your desk as a barricade. Even the best candidate won't give a good impression if he feels he is on the defensive.

3. At the start of the interview, give him an idea of how the interview will go, what ground will be covered, and when he'll get a chance to question you.

4. Skip over the ancient history on the résumé (you can always come back to it) and concentrate on the past five years. Are there missing months or years? Don't be reluctant to ask about them. Now is the time to find out the truth; later will be too late.

5. If he is presently employed, why is he interested in making a change? What does he think of his present employer and the other employees with whom he works? What are his present responsibilities and how do they relate to the position he is applying for? If he is now unemployed, under what conditions did he leave his previous position? What was his relationship with his former employer? Will his former employer give him a strong recommendation? Your objective in asking these questions is to get an indication of his character, his personality, and how he relates to people. If he's negative about previous associations,

consider this to be a flashing red light, a warning signal. It may indicate that he is not the team player you are seeking.

6. Find out whether or not anything motivates him, and if so, what. What aspects of the job give him the greatest satisfaction? What part does he dislike? What in his business life does he regard as his greatest achievement? This line of questioning should tell you several things, the first of which is whether the applicant can think on his feet. (I'd be very wary of someone who had difficulty answering these questions.) Secondly, you should get a clue about how (or if) you will be able to motivate and encourage this applicant if you finally decide to hire him.

7. Your final decision should be based on two questions, which the interview process, if well done, should help you answer easily. How does the applicant stack up against the job? And, if you are favorably inclined towards him, how does he stack up against the other applicants? Don't be afraid of the possibility that, despite having interviewed a mountain of applicants, nobody is quite right. No matter how much of a hurry you think you're in to fill a position, your feeling of urgency can't compare to that sinking feeling you get when you discover that you've hired the wrong person.

8. Please, please, please—check references before you hire anybody. These days many companies, often out of fear of legal action from the discharged individual, are not entirely candid when you inquire about the circumstances under which someone was fired. Thus it really should be a matter of concern when the applicant's references are anything less than complimentary. At the very least, this shows that the applicant is not aware of what others think of him. To me this also indicates a great lack of psychorelations skills.

Giving Out Pink Slips

I may be one of the few executives who hates hiring, but I have lots of company when it comes to hating to fire people. From personal experience I can tell you that firing is *almost* as painful for the employer as for the employee. We executives fidget, hem and haw, sweat, go on pencil-sharpening orgies, and otherwise exhibit bizarre behavior to avoid having to confront this terrible task, a task that will adversely affect the life of another human being. However, that's the way it should be. Firing someone cannot be taken lightly. Those executives who have no problem in wielding the axe over the head, life, and career of another person lack the humility, the kindness, the thoughtfulness, and the sensitivity that I wholeheartedly believe every executive requires if he is to continue to move up the corporate ladder.

Is there a *good* way to fire someone? Well, yes and no. There is most assuredly a *bad* way to fire someone—actually, any number of bad ways. Although I have read books and articles and asked my own management friends, no one has ever convinced me that there is one right time of day, week, or month to fire somebody. Friday afternoons have become the traditional time for handing out walking papers, because both of you—terminator and terminee—have the weekend to recover. Sometimes, however, you just can't win.

One Monday morning Gloria, whom I had personally discharged the previous Friday afternoon with two weeks notice, came in to see me. (I had volunteered to do the deed because no one else was willing to endure the tears that were bound to ensue.) Her visit was brief, but her belligerent message revealed both the pain that she was in and a glimpse of the reasons why we had had to discharge her. Gloria wanted to "advise" me that "next time" I had to fire anybody, Friday afternoon was an "inopportune" time to do so. She had spent the entire weekend crying over the tragedy. I apologized for having ruined her weekend, but found myself wondering what day of the week she might have preferred. Did she resent crying on her own time rather than mine? I don't mean to make light of this situation. Being forced to fire someone is a terrible ordeal for both sides, and you must handle it with the utmost sensitivity and understanding. Maybe that is not your obligation as a boss. It is, however, your obligation as a human being.

Telling the Truth?

When you have to look into those doomed eyes sitting across the desk from you, what do you say? Do you tell the truth or don't you? Although many of my peers disagree, I long ago decided not to tell the whole truth unless the reasons really are purely budgetary. For me, a little white lie is preferable. I find it cruel, thoughtless, harsh, and cold-blooded to tell an employee you are about to fire that he is lazy, not a team player, incompetent, and unable to get along with either his associates or his clients. Most people don't want to know the truth about themselves, and I do not believe it is your obligation to tell them. Why should you twist the knife after you have already stuck it to him?

They aren't likely to believe you anyway. No one accepts that he is being fired because he is incompetent or lazy or is not a team player. Whatever you say and however you say it, it may be twisted around by the discharged employee. You may be accused of firing him for the same reason that Henry Ford II supposedly fired Lee Iacocca. In one of the most famous firings in modern history, Ford, on being asked by Iacocca why he was being fired, allegedly replied, "I just don't like you." Telling the truth, being brutally honest, is like throwing down the gauntlet. Your employee gets defensive and feels obligated to argue every point you have made. Suddenly you find yourself in the middle of World War III. Your job is not to debate him. Your job is to discharge him.

Your approach should be to give your about-to-be discharged employee a reason that precludes the possibility of an argument:

- We are reorganizing the department and unfortunately your job has been eliminated.
- We are making extensive cutbacks, and a group of us were forced to make the decision as to who had to leave.
- When we took you on, we expected that there would be an expansion in your department, but it just doesn't look like that's going to happen.

You may hate to put yourself in the position of stating a little white lie such as this, though there may be a measure of truth in what you say. The person you are firing may not believe you and may even suspect that you are clouding the real truth. Yet this pretense, though transparent to an extent, is far better than destroying a person's sense of self-worth. As the humane boss I hope you are, it is essential that you leave your discharged employee with a degree of self-esteem from which to rebuild his life and livelihood. I would hate to see a fired employee leave my office miserable, dejected, head hanging low on his chest, saying to himself, "I'm a failure."

I would much prefer to have that person leave my office angry at me, saying, "That stupid son of a bitch. I'll get a better job with a bigger salary and he'll realize what an asset I really am. I'll show him what a big mistake he's made in firing me." And it could well be that in the end he'll prove to be right. Many "incompetents" are people who just haven't found the right niche in life.

The public relations field is full of "incompetents" I've fired who have gone on to be successful.

ROGERS' RULES FOR FIRING

1. The golden rule is that all terminations should be carried out with brevity and compassion. Above all, the employee should be the first to know, not the last.

2. Give fair advance warnings, in writing, with specifics. A termination from you should never come as a bolt out of the blue. If you want to give someone a chance to improve, give him a fair chance—tell him what is wrong, and if possible, give him some guidance about how to fix it. If you can, give a time frame within which you expect improvement, and stick to it. Compassion at this point may call for a little white lie. Try taking the blame yourself. You weren't up to giving him the guidance and assistance that his difficult job required. This will permit him to retain his self-respect, which he will need to weather the storm of being fired.

3. Don't permit an argument to ensue. Once the decision has been made, it doesn't do anyone any good to go through a prolonged session in which an employee is permitted to plead for his job.

4. The person being fired will be in real pain—angry, scared, and highly emotional. He will probably not be thinking clearly about the many questions he should ask. Explain that you will do everything you can to help him get another job. Remind him about the severance pay he will be receiving in accordance with company policy. Tell him how long his medical plan will remain in effect and advise him what he should do to protect himself and his family if he is unable to quickly move into another position. Make some suggestions as to what other job opportunities there might be for him. Let him know that you care and that you wish to be helpful.

5. Have a clear agenda of severance arrangements—when to hand in keys, when to leave the building, and all other company policies.

6. Obtain status reports, written or verbal, on any work in progress.

7. If you must fire someone that you yourself hired, this says something about you, too. Did you misjudge him? Was there any way the situation could have been salvaged? Have you learned anything from this experience?

Getting Canned

But suppose the doomed eyes are your own. What if it's you who's been fired? What do you do? What do you say and who do you say it to? Well, it depends on the circumstances. Some businesses are more volatile than others. Short employment is a fact of life in the advertising business, in television . . . and there is always Billy Martin. It may take some doing, but try to be realistic about your situation. Being fired during a pink-slip massacre when heads are rolling all over the office is *not* the same as being fired because your client told your boss to put someone else on his account.

This is the moment in your life when you must be objective, when you must be honest, when you must take off the rose-colored glasses and look at yourself through your boss's eyes. Let's surmise that he's the nice guy I've been describing in the past few pages and he told you that little white lie. Dig down deep into your gut and figure out the real reason why you were fired. Evaluate your own performance. On the scale of one to ten, how do you think he rates you? How do you rate yourself? If there is a discrepancy, what's the reason for it? Does he like you? Does he respect you? What was your relationship with your subordinates, your peers?

Are you wondering why I am asking you to put yourself through this painful self-examination? Because if you can come up with honest, forthright answers, no matter how agonizing they may be for you to admit them, it may open up a whole new world for you. Maybe you have been at fault, maybe your performance has not been as exemplary as you thought it to be. Maybe you didn't work as diligently as you should have. Maybe you were just waltzing through your job thinking it would last forever.

What would you do if you had to do it all over again? Would you have done things differently? Would you have managed your boss differently? Would you have treated your subordinates differently? I find that most people keep making the same mistakes over and over again. They never change, they never learn. "I am what I am," they say to themselves, but I don't accept that. You can get better. You can improve. You can change. Getting fired from this job may be the best thing that ever happened to you. That's up to you, and it all depends on whether you can use this sad and depressing experience as an enlightening one as well.

The best advice I can offer is that you try to grow from the experience. Try to find a way to turn it to your advantage. Many have gone from goat to hero and emerged after being fired more effective than ever before. There are hundreds and thousands of examples all around you of people who were fired from their jobs and went on to great glory and success.

Rogers & Cowan exists today as one of the most respected, most successful public relations firms in the country because a Hollywood publicist named Grace Nolan once fired her twenty-year-old office boy—for incompetence. His name was Henry Rogers. We all have to make our own evaluation as to what constitutes incompetence. For Grace Nolan, incompetence was my forgetting to return her car keys on a Saturday afternoon, leaving her unable to keep an appointment with a prospective client. Was she right? Was she wrong? That is not important today. What is important is that being fired by Grace Nolan turned out to be the most fortunate experience of my life, even though at the time it was for me the greatest tragedy of the twentieth century. I was angry, hurt, resentful, and despondent, the natural reactions of anyone who has just lost his job. When I was unable to get another job, I became an entrepreneur and opened up my own one-man—no secretary publicity office. That is when my career in public relations got under way. Being fired is not a tragedy. Great careers often get under way after one first experiences the drastically emotional experience of looking at a pink slip with your name on it.

ROGERS' RULES FOR BEING FIRED

1. If you can, try to have the presence of mind to ask specifically what you might have done to have salvaged the situation.

2. Don't be vindictive. Now is not the time to sabotage the Xerox machine or run off with all the key files. The worst anyone should say about you is that they're sorry you're gone.

3. Keep your personal feelings about the way your termination was handled to yourself. Keep in mind that musical chairs is a fact of life in almost all businesses. Many people are surprised when their ex-boss shows up at their new office, but it is not all that uncommon. An ill-considered remark can easily follow you from one job to another. The details of your severance agreement should not be shared with co-workers, and the specifics of what was said should stop at your ears and not be repeated. You have nothing to gain and much to lose by giving a blow-by-blow description to others in the office.

How to Quit

When someone makes a decision to quit his job, there is an enormous amount of soul-searching involved. A person has—or at least has the opportunity to have—great security at Rogers & Cowan. Although numerous people have come and gone over the thirty-five years we've been in business, we have a hard core of associates who have remained with our organization for ten, twenty, and twenty-five years. When a person gets restless and begins to think of moving on to greener fields, he wonders whether he's taking too much of a gamble. As I reflect back over the people who have passed through our organization, there is no consistent pattern. Some talented people who left us have never been heard of again. I can only assume they would have been better off if they had decided to stay.

On the other hand, one day we will have a reunion of our "alumni"—those who quit Rogers & Cowan and went on to greater achievements. Guy McElwaine, after a circuitous path through theatrical agencies and movie production companies, recently resigned as chairman and chief executive officer of Columbia Pictures. John Foreman was able to capitalize on his ability to relate to actors and became a highly respected producer, responsible for *Butch Cassidy and the Sundance Kid, The Man Who Would Be King,* and *Prizzi's Honor,* among others. David Foster, who started as a trainee in our television department, went on to independent film production and was associated with such outstanding movies as *McCabe and Mrs. Miller, The Getaway,* and *The Drowning Pool.* Jay Bernstein is a highly respected personal manager and the producer of the "Mike Hammer" television series.

Others who left us stayed in public relations, among them Robert Marston in corporate PR and Warren Cavior in investor relations. On the Hollywood scene, Dick Guttman, Jim Mahoney, and Pat Kingsley are just a few who have gone on to great success on their own.

Who should quit his secure job and who shouldn't? A person has to feel confident that he can do better elsewhere, and if he has that confidence he should take a deep breath and dive into the icy waters of uncertainty. It only hurts once. Having people leave our company is an unpleasant experience for us as the employers. It is an inconvenience and sometimes impedes our continuing growth. Yet we have a complete understanding for those who feel they can better their careers by moving elsewhere. If someone who is respected in the organization leaves, the best approach is to take it in pleasant stride. We would rather have a valued employee stay, but when the new job is an opportunity and a step up that we can't match, we always make it a point to send them off with flowers and champagne.

Kathie Berlin, who, as mentioned earlier, headed up our New York Entertainment division for twelve years, recently resigned to go into television production with Marlo Thomas and Carol Hart. She gave us two months advance notice that she was about to make the change. She told the many, many of our clients with whom she had been involved that she was leaving and impressed upon each of them that she had left an efficient team behind her, schooled in her image, and she was confident that their needs would be well taken care of. Finally, she told each of the clients that she would be available at no cost for consultation with any of them who might want to meet with her for the first six months that she was away. This was an ideal transitional situation, one that is founded on the ongoing respect that employer and employee had built up over the years.

To Quit or Not To Quit

Are you now tempted to quit your job? Should you or shouldn't you? It's not an easy question to answer, and you will have a tremendous advantage if you have someone you can confide in. This is a difficult answer to arrive at by yourself. I'm not advising you to automatically *accept* someone else's advice. No. In contrast, I suggest that you just *listen* to someone else's point of view, because it can be the best or the worst decision of your life.

Talk to someone. It may be a person in the office whom you trust, it may be your spouse, it may be your best friend, your father, mother, brother, sister, son, daughter, banker, lawyer— anyone with whom you enjoy a rapport.

Tell him or her your story, but don't give the impression that you want agreement. Tell your confidante that you have not made a decision as yet. What does he or she think you should do? You don't want a yes man at this point; you want a devil's advocate. This is a decision you will eventually make alone, but before making it listen to the other side of the story.

Once you have made up your mind to quit your job, and you are convinced that your decision has been made on the basis of sound business principles rather than sheer emotionalism, you are faced with another problem. Do you quit before you have found another job, or do you look for another job first? That's easy. Don't quit your job. You're a more desirable prospect for a new employer if you continue working.

At one time we were looking for a chief administrative officer for our company, and through word of mouth, we came across someone we liked. He was at the time the number-two man in the administration and finance department of a large Los Angeles law firm. One of the senior partners of that firm is one of my very close friends.

"Do you mind if I talk with Dick Sherwood about you?" I asked at our first meeting.

"Not at all," he replied. "They know that I'm looking for a number-one position, and they are willing to let me look while I'm still holding down my job with them."

That of course is the ideal circumstance under which you should be looking for another job—but unfortunately, there aren't too many situations as favorable as that. Unless your boss is an unusually understanding person whom you trust implicitly, it is my advice that you should not confide in him.

Once you have made the decision to look for another position, don't allow your present work to become slipshod. This is difficult to achieve, for it takes a Herculean endeavor to keep up your normal pace at the office while simultaneously casting about for a new career opportunity. It is important to accomplish both objectives simultaneously for a number of reasons. First, as an employer, I feel very strongly that you owe your boss the same honest day's work that you have always given him. You have made your own decision about a career change, and there is no reason why he should suffer by your giving him a four-hour day instead of your normal eight-hour day. Maybe you can get away with it and no one will be the wiser, but there is a more important consideration to think about. You have a moral obligation. I believe the moral issue here is an important one, but that's for you to decide.

If you continue to work your normal eight-hour day as I have recommended, you must then ask, "When do I get the time to look for another job?" This is where networking comes in. Yes, networking. Confide in a friend. Ask him to confide in another friend, who in turn will mention you and your dilemma to someone else. Have lunch with someone who is in another position. Have a drink at the end of the day with an acquaintance. Use Saturdays and Sundays.

It is important for me to stress here that this is the network process. You are not yet job hunting. You are *not* looking for a job. Let me explain. You have a job. You can remain in that job for the rest of your life. Then why are you networking? Because you are ambitious, you are aggressive, and you want to make more of your life. You are asking for advice. You would like to kick some ideas around. On this basis, everyone's door is open to you. Everyone will welcome the opportunity to meet with you. Why? Because you are asking for something that everyone is not only willing but anxious to give—advice. From this advice an ideal new job opportunity may open up. It may; it may not.

Finally the day will arrive when your boss calls you in and says, "Joe, I hear that you have been out job hunting." Be prepared for this confrontation. Don't let it come as surprise to you. As careful as you have been with your networking, there is always a good chance that it will get back to your boss. You have a number of alternatives. None of them involves lying.

Tell him that you have not been job hunting, but that you are thinking about a career change. You have been asking the advice of friends, but you have meticulously continued to do your job as you always have. Keep the conversation on an impersonal level. If one of the reasons you are contemplating a change is your incompatibility with your boss, don't bring that up as a reason.

If he brings it up, deny it, telling him that people who work together don't necessarily have to be playpen pals. This is an important point to make, because if you allow your personal differences with him to become a factor, it becomes a psychological defeat for him, and that is a disadvantageous position for you to be in.

Your objective at this point is to keep the conversation on such pleasant terms that he will ask you to stay on and continue with your duties while you are exploring other opportunities. However, let's face it. This is rare, and don't be surprised if he shows a lack of compassion and understanding and asks you to clear out your desk and be out of the office by the end of the day. That's the gamble you must make when you decide to quit your job. There are certain risks involved and you should be aware of them before you decide that a career change is in order. Make sure you know what you're getting into before you take the big step.

ROGERS' RULES FOR QUITTER'S ETIQUETTE

1. If you're job hunting, you still owe your current employer the same honest day's work that you've always given him. Job hunt on your own time, not your boss's time. This is difficult to do, but don't expect empathy or understanding from your boss if he discovers that you arrived at your office at ten-thirty this morning because you were out on a job interview.

2. Rehearse for the possible confrontation when your boss says, "I hear you've been job hunting." Don't admit that you're looking for a new job. You are just exploring new career opportunities. Your goal is to continue looking for a job at your convenience, not his.

3. Be as helpful as you can in finding a replacement to fill your spot. Suggest names of people who might be qualified for your job.

4. Burn no bridges. Even if you are leaving because of a personality conflict with your boss, keep open the possibility of

returning to the corporation sometime in the future. Imagine what would happen if the boss who you find to be offensive left your company and a dream boss were hired instead. If you leave in a huff, the company records will still remember you as an "undesirable" long after the reason for your unhappiness has departed.

8

Troublesome and Troubled People

You'll find them in every organization, large or small. They're the mavericks, the renegades, the black sheep, the prima donnas, the weirdos, the kooks. Some never grew up; some have emotional problems. Some have uncontrollable tempers; some appear to lack sound business judgment. With others, irrational behavior seems to be the norm rather than the exception. Yet for a great many reasons, they continue to hold responsible positions, and it is your responsibility to work with them.

Why are they given special treatment? How can they continue to exhibit behavior that obviously isn't tolerated in others? One may be the boss's nincompoop son; another, for some unknown reason, may be a sacred cow. One may have started in business with the boss fifty years ago and must be accommodated. For the most part, however, there is a very good, logical reason: *talent.*

Most people in any organization are competent, but there is a big difference between competence and talent. The competent folk are those who know how to put one foot in front of the other, who turn out a reliable, acceptable—if unremarkable—work product. There are certain mavericks, however, who must be tolerated and accommodated because they hear that "different drum" that results in true innovation and distinguishes them from all the rest of us. When one of these troublesome and troubled people appears on the scene, management hangs in there and asks you to play along. Despite the trouble they cause, mavericks often come up with the big play that makes it all worthwhile. They're the people management loves to hate.

There is also the inertia factor. Some less talented mavericks are able to survive because of the natural inertia that exists in all organizations. No one wants to take on the task of firing them and finding a replacement. Tolerance for mavericks fluctuates with cyclical swings in business. When business gets tough, it gets tougher on the mavericks. When profits are increasing dramatically, management has a much easier time closing the corporate eyes to individual idiosyncracies.

IBM, General Motors, Xerox, and other industrial giants never did succumb to pressures to ease up on their ultraconservative dress and appearance codes. Those who resisted the dress code had a difficult time of it, but even the great General Motors made an exception for an exceptional maverick in those days. Long before his troubles with cocaine, when the FBI brought him to the attention of every newspaper in the world, John DeLorean caused heads to turn in the executive offices of company headquarters because of his flowing, carefully coiffed hair and his flamboyant clothes. Heads turned, but DeLorean's star continued to shine brighter for many years at GM, simply because as general manager of the Pontiac division and subsequently as the big boss of Chevrolet, he was responsible for hundreds of millions of dollars in profits for the parent company.

He and the board of directors finally agreed to disagree and he left the company, but during his many years of employment there, his nonconformist appearance and behavior were reluctantly accepted.

What is the moral of this story? Bring sufficient profits to the company and you can get away with almost anything. What is the Rogers' Rules corollary to this moral? Make sure you are profitable to the company *before* you show your true maverick stripes. When the profits are not quite as rosy as they once were, don't expect the maverick behavior to be accepted forever.

Don't get the idea that the key to success is to become a rebel—a Trotskyite or an anarchist. As much as business may tolerate the brilliant eccentric, the "normal" talented person has a much easier time of it. But how do *you* deal with the mavericks? Suppose one of them is your boss?

Coping with Mr. Tirade

Mavericks come in many different varieties, but one of the most difficult to deal with is Mr. Tirade, the person who blows up and begins screaming and yelling—at you or whomever else is handy—when something goes wrong. He can turn the novice or the marginal incompetent into a sniveling neurotic by continually harping at him, standing over his desk, and swearing at his mistakes. Even the competent and talented feel his wrath when things go wrong, and everything that goes wrong *must* be blamed on someone. (That someone, by the way, is never him.)

It's not only difficult, it's demoralizing and stressful to work with someone like this. Working for such a person can make any job sheer drudgery. What do you do?

There is no one answer to that question. First, you must decide if working for him is worth the price. Does the job pay enough for you to accept the beating you are forced to take? Can you see a way out? Is there a possibility that you will be moved out of his department in the near future? Might there also be a possibility that he will move on to another department or another company? Once you decide that the job is worth the anguish involved, then you must devise a system where emotionally, at least, you're in charge—even though your boss will never know it. Accept the fact that he will never change, or at least that *you* will never be able to change him. The secret is to learn to control yourself—and "take charge."

This was exemplified for me one day when Jerry, a young executive friend of mine, was telling me about his boss, who was irrational and out of control a good percentage of the time. "Why do you take it?" I asked him.

Jerry laughed. "Oh, I know how to handle him. I don't pay any attention to his ranting and raving, and I ignore his blustering memos. I just do my job the way I know it should be done, knowing that I'm too valuable to the company for him to demand a confrontation. It's not the best of all worlds, but I find it to be a fascinating challenge. In fact," he added thoughtfully, "I think I thrive on it. It's like playing a game, but he doesn't know that it's going on. I'm the only player."

You may not want to live your life the way Jerry does, but this is an excellent example of someone "taking charge" without his boss being aware of it. Taking charge, of course, means taking charge of yourself. You have a great advantage if you can manage to remember Rudyard Kipling's advice and "keep your head while those about you are losing theirs." It is not a sign of weakness to bend, if that is what the situation calls for, but when you do bend, do it with dignity. Don't become a doormat, a toady. If you do, you will lose all respect, not only from your boss but from your peers—and, most importantly, from yourself as well.

There may come a time when you decide to summon up every ounce of courage you have and make a stand. It's not easy, because your job may be at stake. Only you can make that decision. Are you willing to take that gamble? Each of us has his own tolerance level, and you must decide for yourself the degree to which you will permit yourself to be pushed before you say, as did Peter Finch as Howard Beale in *Network*, "I'm mad as hell and I'm not going to take it anymore."

If you decide to make a stand, there is a way to do it properly. Pick a time when conditions are comparatively quiet and ask to see him.

"Mr. Tirade," you should start by saying, "I have a good position and I want to stay here. I know that you have a tough job and that you work under a lot of pressure, but I must ask you to show me some degree of respect. I'm sure you don't realize how you speak to me at times. If you expect a high level of performance from me, try to realize that the better I am treated, the better the job I will be able to do for you."

I won't guarantee it, but I am reasonably certain that a short speech like that will get a favorable response from him. Why do I think so? Because without even knowing you, I am certain that he needs you more than you need him. With his irrational behavior, he cannot be surrounded by a particularly strong team, and he doesn't want to lose you. As long as you realize that he cannot do his job without you, you should have no fear about asserting yourself. As a friend of mine once said, "The meek shall inherit the earth, but only if they assert themselves."

What if I'm wrong? Two things can happen. Either he will ignore your request and you will be right back where you started, or there is a remote possibility that he will fly into a rage and fire you. If you aren't willing to take that minor risk then you are probably better off living with Mr. Tirade for the rest of your life and making the best of it.

ROGERS' RULES FOR COPING WITH MR. TIRADE

1. Try to analyze Mr. Tirade's patterns of behavior. If you discover that certain situations and conditions light his short fuse, make certain that you are not the one who lights it. If someone else sets him off, try to stay away from him during his emotional explosions.

2. If he blows up at you, think of the tirade as a thunderstorm. Thunderstorms are intense but short-lived. He can't yell for long. He will exhaust himself. In the meantime, control yourself. Do not interrupt; do not yell back in return. Wait for the squall to subside, then excuse yourself from his presence. Later, in a calm moment a day or two later, bring up the subject again. Maybe this time he can discuss it with you rationally and intelligently. Don't mention the previous thunderstorm.

3. Try to put yourself on an equal physical footing with him as soon as the tirade begins. If he is towering over you, yelling, interrupt for a moment to suggest politely that he take a seat. He might ignore your suggestion, but he just might do it. If you are standing in front of his desk, ask, also politely, "May I sit down?" Just the act of both of you sitting may create a break in the action and give you a chance to recoup your composure.

4. If he is playing out the scenario in front of other members of the company, gently suggest that it might be best for the two of you to conduct your impending conversation—or his mono-logue—alone. I caution you—be gentle. There is no assurance that he won't be too far out of control to listen to your recom-mendations.

5. Do not directly contradict him. This will set off another thunderstorm, accompanied by flashes of lightning and small craft warnings. This is the time for a sidestep, a time-out, a postponement. Acknowledge the gravity of the issue and either ask permission to tell your version of the story or ask for time to

double-check the information he has just given you or you have just given him.

6. Eventually, after the storm has passed, the next day or the next week, ask for a meeting and talk out the problems that were previously discussed with emotion and hysteria. Mr. Tirade, by that time, may be ashamed of the way he acted, or he may even have forgotten about it. Even if he begins to apologize, discount any fault in his behavior. No one was right, no one was wrong. Talk it out, air the problems, but stay away from personal criticism. Keep your speech clear of loaded words and phrases that are bound to make him bristle: "The trouble with you is . . ."; "You always . . ."; "It's not fair that you . . ."; "You think that . . ." Never tell him what he thinks. That will only set him off again.

Coping with a Difficult Boss

Fortunately, most bosses are not Mr. Tirades. If they were, many of us would wind up in the looney bin. There are thousands of you, however, who are having trouble with your bosses, even though they are probably normal human beings. You may find your boss difficult to work for, but before you spend a lot of time criticizing him, I suggest that you take a good look at yourself first.

Are you doing your job as well as you can? Are his standards higher than yours? Is he justified in being as demanding as he is? Should you place one hundred percent of the blame for your unpleasant relationship on his shoulders, or might you be partially to blame?

Let's start with the assumption that you just don't know how to manage him and that if you can learn how, then the bulk of your problems will disappear.

Let's start from the beginning. What does he expect of you?

What are your job responsibilities? What does he want you to report to him on, and what doesn't he want to be bothered with? If you are like most people in middle management, it is most likely that you have never come to an understanding with your boss on these key matters. You came to work one day, he showed you where your desk was, and you started to work. Very little indoctrination, very few if any ground rules, no discussion of his likes or dislikes, no serious discussion of how the two of you should work together.

If this is your case, I would like you to start all over again. Tell your boss that even though you have been working together for quite some time, there are certain areas of authority and responsibility about which you are not clear and you would like to meet with him to discuss them. If you can manage it, try to get him away from his desk. Ask if you can take him to lunch. He may just agree, and if he does, you have already scored an important point. You have established that you are about to have a serious discussion that is worth his serious attention. Now that you have set yourself up properly, what's the next step? *Get prepared.*

Spend the evening before your scheduled meeting making up a list of subjects that need to be clarified—these subjects may be clear to him, but they are muddled to you. You need clarification from him. You may want to redo your list of questions three or four times before you're satisfied. Why are they so important? Because if you can get satisfactory answers, many of your present job problems will disappear.

What do you want to accomplish through your upcoming meeting?

1. You want to satisfy his needs as well as your own.
2. You want to know exactly what he expects of you.
3. You must satisfy yourself that you can meet his expectations.

4. Does he want your opinion after he has given you a directive? Find out.
5. Does he expect you to agree with everything he says?
6. Learn his work habits in relationship to you. Will he see you any time you want to meet with him, or does he prefer to set up a specific appointment in advance?
7. Does he want you to work directly with him or funnel everything through his secretary?
8. What does he like and dislike about your work habits? What changes can he recommend?
9. How does he wish you to report to him?
10. Does he prefer verbal or written reports? Short or long?
11. Does he prefer that you keep his work hours? Earlier? Later? Weekends?

Before you start, tell him the purpose of the meeting and that you have prepared a list of questions, the answers to which will help you do a better job for him. Tell him that you will be making notes so that you'll remember what has been agreed upon.

Your meeting is finished. I predict that it will have been an enormous success. Your boss will appreciate your interest in improving your relationship. You're sure that you have now solved all your problems. Not at all. You're just beginning. Study your notes intently, because you now have to interpret what was said. Earlier in this book I dealt with communication. I wrote that people often find it difficult to say what they really mean, and the listener finds it equally difficult to determine not only what the other person said, but what he meant to say. After you have studied your notes, condense them to a concise list, "Things to Remember." Take it home that night and study it. Then place it in your desk drawer and look at it two or three times a day until you have memorized all the rules you have established for yourself on *how to manage your boss.*

You will find that this procedure will pay off for you in a hundred ways. You will begin to enjoy your job. The tensions between you and your boss will lessen tremendously—and you will find that your own job performance will be greatly improved.

When You Can't Cope with a Difficult Boss

If you have gone through all of this and find that your boss is still impossible to deal with, you are faced with a decision that will affect your entire life. You can sit back and take it, thereby accepting a job of drudgery and unpleasantness for an indefinite period of time, or you can ready yourself for a confrontation.

Confrontations are horrendous experiences. Many people can't handle them. Others thrive on them. For those who can't cope with them, sweeping the problem under the rug is easier than bringing it out into the open.

Eventually you might come to the decision that you just don't want to take it anymore. You don't want to live your life constantly being criticized, constantly being badgered and second-guessed. There will come a moment when you say, "I can't manage my boss." If it comes to that, you just have to make up your mind as to whether you are ready to make the big break. If you decide that you are, do it logically and without anger, if that is possible. You never know when you might change your mind and ask to get your old job back. Try to make the big break as unemotional and as professional as possible.

But suppose you decide to stick it out. Suppose you realize and accept that your boss is a troublesome or even a troubled person, but despite that, you might still have the best job in town. You know that you can't manage him, but you can improve your relationship with him by handling and attempting to work with him in a more intelligent manner. Here are a few tips that might prove helpful.

ROGERS' RULES FOR HANDLING YOURSELF WHEN YOU GET ANGRY WITH YOUR BOSS

Don't explode. Keep cool. Control your temper. Think—count to ten.

By the time you count to ten, you will have calmed down. You will still need time, however, to think through what your position should be. You don't want to offend your boss even though he may have offended you. Get out of his office; it's time for a break. Excuse yourself gently and politely. "I'm very upset," you can say to him. "I'd like to go back to my office and think this over. Once I have it straightened out in my mind, I'd like to come back and review our discussion." If you have any kind of relationship with your boss at all, he will respect this intelligent approach and will patiently await your return.

Once you are back in your own office and have calmed down a bit, it's time to ask yourself

- Why am I angry?
- Is my anger justified?
- What do I want from him at this point? An apology? If he offers it, accept it graciously. If he doesn't, how important is it that he apologize to you? An apology will satisfy your ego needs. Is it essential that your ego needs be satisfied? Is it important enough to turn this issue into a major production?

Think it through. What is to be gained from a confrontation? I am not suggesting that you avoid a confrontation. That is your decision to make. I am asking you to weigh the pros and cons. What do you have to gain? What do you have to lose?

Once you have weighed your alternatives and realize what is at stake when you return to the boss's office, you are ready to resume the meeting you were having when your anger brought the meeting to a halt. Going in, remember that you already have an advantage. You stopped before you blew up, before an explosive situation developed. You handled yourself effectively and with admirable decorum.

Coping with a Difficult Employee

Dealing with difficult people, whether they be bosses or employees, is another example of the One-Hat Solution at work. For the most part, the same rules apply.

As a boss, you are faced with numerous problems every day. The higher up the corporate ladder you progress, the more numerous become the problems. One of the most common and challenging to handle is the talented but difficult subordinate. He complicates your life. He frustrates you. He gets you angry. If he weren't so talented, you would get rid of him.

With the talented but difficult person, however, you face a formidable problem. First, is it worth having someone complicate your life to such a great extent and keep you in such a state of anger and frustration? Yes, it's worth it up to a point, but because he is a key member of your team it is doubtful that you will ever throw up your hands and say "I can't handle him anymore." To make certain that you never arrive at that point, there is only one solution for you: *learn to cope.*

Let me try to label some of the talented but difficult employees

I have encountered over the years and how I have attempted to cope with them.

The Defier of Authority

He knows he's good. He can't be bothered with following the rules. He goes his own way. We gave him authority a long time ago, but he's like an undisciplined kid. We gave him an ice cream cone and he took over the whole Baskin-Robbins shop. Yet no one cares more—no one works harder or is more devoted. What to do?

I spend time with him. I don't lecture him. I don't scold him. We have pleasant breakfast and luncheon appointments. I tell him about company problems. I discuss fiscal responsibility with him. I make him feel that he is a key member of the firm. The result? I know that I'm getting through. He is less difficult, more responsible than he was last year and the year before. What has happened to me during that time? I feel gratified because I feel I have made headway. I am less frustrated than I was before. I don't get angry because for the most part he has stopped doing many of the things that used to provoke my anger. I have learned to cope with him. You must do the same with talented members of your team who tend to defy authority.

The Complainer

He comes in every day with a complaint about something or someone. The air conditioning isn't working properly. He resents the way a client just spoke to him. His secretary makes too many mistakes. The man next door blows cigar smoke in his face. The accounting department hasn't reimbursed him yet for his expense account. The complaints go on and on. I *cope*.

I listen. I take him seriously. I let him know that I care and that I am concerned about his problems. But I try not to indulge him. I explain to him that none of us are perfect and that we all make mistakes. I tell him about a mistake I made last week. I suggest to him that he talk to our office manager about the air conditioning in his office. I suggest that he discuss with our controller the problem of getting quicker action when he submits his expense account. I tell him that I'll talk to the man who blows cigar smoke in his face. I suggest to him how he can solve the "problems" that generate his complaints, and I even offer to solve them myself. He usually leaves my office in a much more pleasant state of mind than when he walked in.

The Clam

A man with a face like Chief Thundercloud goes by your office. When you see him at the water cooler and ask, "What's wrong?" he says, "Nothing," and walks away. There seems to be at least one in every office: the Clam. Consider yourself fortunate if he or she is a subordinate. If it's your boss, you've got some real problems.

The Clam Complex can have any number of causes, but one of them is shyness. Shy people often put on a gruff, uncommunicative facade to hide their fears. "If I'm quiet enough," they think, "no one will want to talk to me and then I won't have to come out of my shell." Other people, like me, have or have had speech problems (I stuttered as a youth) and consequently are afraid of embarrassing themselves if they speak up. Without being the company therapist, it is your job as a middle manager to draw out the uncommunicative, both above you and below you.

Clams deserve the same attention from middle management as

their more gregarious associates. It is easier to leave them alone to make their own way in the organization, but if you do, you're doing a disservice to them, your company, and yourself. With a little care, nurturing, and feeding, plus "tea and sympathy," the Clam can be pried open, and if and when that happens, his true abilities and talents are given the opportunity to shine.

We have Clams in our organization, and I have found that the way to get them to open up is to pursue them. I know they will never make a move in my direction. They will never walk into my office and say, "Will you help me to solve this problem please?" It is not their nature, and I don't expect it of them. I must be the aggressor.

It's not easy because my attempts to develop a personal relationship are often met with suspicion, caution, almost resentment. I can sometimes imagine that he is saying to himself, "Why doesn't the boss leave me alone? What does he want from me?" I feel that I must persist despite early rejection.

Again, I have found some techniques that have worked for me. You might try them even though we know that each clam is unique and requires unique treatment. If these don't work, then they might give you a clue as to how you can develop your own approach to Clams who work for you.

ROGERS' RULES FOR OPENING CLAMS

1. You go first. Initiate a conversation. Don't make it a formal appointment or meeting.

2. Keep your encounters light. Talk about sports, the weather, their families—make them feel comfortable with you.

3. Consider cornering them. The lunch room, the water cooler, even the rest room is fair game. (You have trapped them there; they have to say something.)

4. Don't put them on the spot. If you know Alfred is afraid of speaking, don't ask him to attend a meeting and turn to him and say "Alfred, tell us what you think." You'll scare him out of a year's growth.

5. Help the reluctant communicator along. If Alice has finally worked up the courage to come into your office and is beating around the bush, make it easy for her. Say, "I imagine you want to discuss what happened at the client presentation on Tuesday."

The Salieri—To Cope or Not to Cope

The Salieri is more difficult to cope with—and more dangerous, because you don't know what he's going to do, or when, or to whom. This kind of individual doesn't believe he can be a success unless others around him fail. And so he stacks the deck against his associates, playing mean little games in the hope that this will further his advancement at the expense of others. He does this because in his heart of hearts he fears that he really isn't as good as those around him. The world-class prototype of this individual is Antonio Salieri, Mozart's nemesis in real life, whom you may have seen portrayed in the film *Amadeus*. Salieri was a conniver, a plotter, a deceitful person who could not stand the fact that Mozart was more talented than he was. Under the guise of friendship, he set out to destroy Mozart, and succeeded.

The problem you face with the Salieri in your organization is to decide whether it pays to cope with him. How talented is he? How productive is he? How profitable is he to the company? How do the pros stack up against the cons? That's the problem only you can answer. My experience is that you should not try to cope with proven Salieris.

ROGERS' RULES FOR SALIERI PREVENTION

1. Mind the store. It's an old expression but a good one. Watch carefully what goes on around you. Delegate authority and responsibility, as you must, but know what everyone is doing. It's much harder for someone to sabotage you if you are in tune with what's happening.

2. Keep your eyes and ears open. If you notice a change in the way people in the office treat you, something's up. Don't ignore those signs. Get to the bottom of the change. Pin people down. Ask questions.

3. Be wary of people with bad track records or even one case that smacks of betrayal.

4. Don't make yourself a victim by waiting for a *fait accompli*. Once a decision unfavorable to you is down in black and white, it will be too late. If you believe that an associate is trying to undermine you, make a preemptive strike and argue your case with the higher-ups. This is a difficult situation. You don't wish to look petty, but it is important that you protect yourself. My recommendation is that you alert your superior to what you believe is happening. Ask him to take no action, but say that you felt that you had an obligation to bring the matter to his attention.

6. Build bridges in your company with people at all levels—your associates, your employees, and your boss. Mozart unwittingly helped Salieri by antagonizing many potential allies. Salieris have a much easier time with anonymous or unpopular victims than with those who are well known and well liked.

Coping With the Basket Case

There comes a time in everyone's life when his work suffers because of problems that have nothing to do with the office. That time may have already come in your life. I know it has happened to me on a number of occasions over the years. Divorce or separation, a death in the family, or a joyous occasion like a new baby can bring temporary instability and a lapse in productivity to even the most competent and even-tempered person.

When your boss or one of your subordinates temporarily experiences an emotional trauma, accept it philosophically. Don't complain. Find a way to compensate, to fill the void. Give him a chance to bounce back. Most likely he will.

The people we call "Basket Cases" are something else again. They are people who live life on an emotional roller coaster. Like a character trapped in a soap opera, the Basket Case is always involved in some personal crisis. He is not happy unless he is mixed up with an emotional problem involving himself, his family, or his friends. If there isn't a crisis available at the moment, he will find one—or create one. There are long personal telephone conversations with family and friends, some tearful, some somber, some angry. Tardiness and absenteeism become a way of life as personal problems overwhelm office responsibilities. Superiors, co-workers, and subordinates have no choice but to pick up the pieces until the crisis is over, at least until the next time.

I've seen it in all kinds of people, men and women, young and old. Basket Cases get hooked on the melodrama of their lives. Without meaning to, they go out of their way to create these disasters for themselves, because it's more interesting to live this kind of emotional life than an "ordinary" one of stability. Dealing sympathetically with a Basket Case is particularly difficult because it's easy to get sucked into the melodrama yourself. I've had employees with whom it was a real act of bravery to ask, "How are you?"

Why? Because they would begin to tell me—and then I would

be forced to listen to a mini-version of the heartrending Perils of Paul or Pauline.

I remember Melissa dragging herself melodramatically out of my office, having just taken fifteen minutes to explain how she had just suffered her third minor traffic accident in as many months and now her insurance was going to be canceled and not only that but she was breaking up with her boyfriend and her poodle was at the vet with cataracts and—I'll spare you the rest.

"Melissa's going through a tough time," I said to one of my associates.

"For heaven's sake don't humor her," came the stinging reply. "Melissa is a walking disaster area. It's just one thing after another. In the beginning I was sympathetic, but there's just no end to it. We all feel sorry for her, but if we let her she would spend the whole day telling us about her life. No one would ever get anything done. You can't tell me she's working as hard as the rest of us in the department. She's too busy feeling sorry for herself."

"I guess it's time to have a talk with her," I said reluctantly.

"You're right. I'm afraid that our tolerance is encouraging her to continue."

I went to see Melissa in her office later that day. As gently as I could I told her that I thought her problems were affecting her job performance and that of others around her. All of us, I assured her, have personal problems, but most of us manage to put them away during office hours.

Melissa looked at me as if I had just added one more trouble to her already overburdened psyche. She didn't understand. "But who else can I tell my troubles to?" In an instant I had turned from being a sympathetic ear to being an additional source of angst. I left her office feeling both guilty and frustrated—guilty because she made me feel like I'd genuinely hurt her feelings, frustrated because it seemed like I'd done it for nothing.

A few weeks later, Melissa resigned without an explanation. I'm sure she believed that we didn't care enough about her to be her "friends" and listen to her pour out her soul to us. We did care, but only up to a point. She had asked us to go beyond that point. I've since lost track of her, but I certainly hope her life is less complicated now than it was then.

ROGERS' RULES FOR BASKET CASES

1. Before acting, be sure that you have a genuine Basket Case, not just someone who's temporarily having a rough time. Everyone is entitled to some emotional ups and downs, but having them too often is a sign for you to take action.

2. If the Basket Case is a subordinate, gently but kindly get them out of the "oh poor me" mode. Try to generate sympathy—even guilt—about how their difficulties are affecting others. Say, "I know you've been going through a tough time lately, but Jenny had to work through the weekend to get that report of yours out on time."

3. If that approach doesn't work, you must take more severe measures. Suggest counseling or other psychological help. Although your subordinate may be insulted by the thought, for some melodrama addicts just the suggestion that they need help may shake them out of their difficulties.

4. The rules are different if the Basket Case is your boss. His condition is an opportunity for you. Become his father or mother confessor if the chance arises. Volunteer to help with his workload. Such action might be stressful and tedious, but it will enhance your career. At worst he will appreciate your help and recommend an increase for you at the next salary review. At best you may be putting yourself in a position to take over his job. You are learning his job, being a team player, and carrying out your own responsibilities at the same time. How can you lose?

Coping with the Cliff Hanger

The completion of each and every project is a real nail-biting affair. No matter how much advance notice is given, "Last-Minute Charlie" is always going down to the wire. He's mobilizing everyone in the office, pulling other projects out of secretarial typewriters, saying imperiously, "Agnes, this is a rush. I'm on deadline. Start typing on page eleven of the manuscript. Carol over in accounting is working on pages one through five. Sue in research has pages six through ten. We'll work through the weekend if necessary."

The hell of it is that most of the time he gets away with it. His stuff really is good. For whatever reason, Charlie really does work better with that surge of adrenaline that hits him as he nears his deadline. Everyone, however, pays the price. His tardiness disrupts the orderly flow of work in the office. Turnover is likely to be higher in his section than elsewhere. And sooner or later, his crisis mentality pushes everyone into the pressure cooker. The underlying attitude, which is not too hard to read, is "My work is more important than yours. Get out of my way."

His attitude used to drive me crazy, and only his ability saved him. The conventional wisdom is to give the Cliff Hanger fake deadlines, but this will not change his habits; it will just make the crisis happen earlier. What do you do?

ROGERS' RULES FOR DEADLINE AVOIDERS

1. If the offender is a subordinate, give him a deadline with plenty of time to complete the project. Then begin a program of "constructive hounding." Drop into his office a few days after the assignment is given and ask if he needs any help. In particular ask if he'll need any extra manpower to complete the project.

2. A few days before deadline, ask if he wants to give you a status report or show you a rough draft.

3. Start off "dealing day" by asking what time you can expect completion. If the day passes without evidence that the project has been completed, give him another day but warn him that this is his last chance. If one more day goes by, take the project away from him and reassign it to someone else.

4. If the offender is an associate, offer help early in the project, but make yourself unavailable as the deadline draws near. The deadline avoider continues in this pattern at least partly because he never really has to confront the negative consequences of his own work habits.

The Ix-nayer

If Orville and Wilbur had listened to this one, we'd still be taking the train from New York to Los Angeles. His favorite expression is, "It'll never get off the ground." A skillful and talented individual himself, he is always ready to torpedo any new idea, or at least any new idea from someone other than himself. Eventually his negativism is paralyzing and the new ideas stop coming forth at all. What's the use? Everyone knows what's going to happen to any new suggestion. Morale drops $12\frac{1}{2}$ percent and everyone who has to work with this individual appears to be wallowing in despair. What's needed here is someone who can change the negative to the positive. Why not you? Optimism is at least as contagious as pessimism.

ROGERS' RULES FOR PESSIMISTS

1. Keep a positive attitude. Don't get drawn into the gloom.

2. Get the problem clearly defined and fully out in the open. In explaining why something won't work, Ix-nayers often make more of the problem than there really is.

3. Without contradicting the Ix-nayer, present a range of alternative solutions. Steal a page from the military and adopt a "worst case" stance. Compare the most dire consequences of any alternative action to the most dire consequences of doing nothing. How bad can it be?

4. Use a little humor, if you can. It's much easier to look on the positive side of any situation with a smile on your face.

Coping with Troublesome and Troubled People

Do you remember the halcyon, carefree days before you were elevated to the ranks of middle management? It was easy. All you had to think about was your own job and getting along reasonably well with the people around you. Life was simple. Now look. It's tough enough to handle your own workload, but you spend half your time handling people—and no one warned you that many of them would be troublesome or troubled people. Is it worth it? Only you can make that decision, but I have a hunch that if you have taken the time to read this book, you decided a long time ago that it is.

Just remember that if one day you move up into your boss's

present position, it will get tougher, not easier. Understand too that the higher up the corporate ladder you move, the more complex the problems become, the heavier the workload. Then why do so many of you want to move up? Because of the challenge, the excitement, the sense of accomplishment, the natural desire to do better than your neighbor. It's a worthwhile struggle. That's why so many of us would like to be president of the United States.

9

Motivating Your Employees and Managing Your Boss

In the introduction, we established that as a middle manager, you hold two positions and have two sets of responsibilities. You have a boss to manage and a staff of subordinates who must be motivated as well as managed. Although you wear two hats, one as a subordinate and one as a boss, you could and should live your business life more efficiently and more comfortably. As one person, you should not try to change hats. Wear the same one as you approach each of your two responsibilities.

The two jobs, despite a number of minor variations, are very much alike. You have specific responsibilities to the guy on top as well as to those who report to you. Your behavior and actions should command respect, and if you are liked as well as respected, you are two or three or ten steps ahead. You are required to instill certain work habits in your employees to inspire them to their highest performance level. Simultaneously, your own work performance is supposed to impress your boss to the extent that one day he will recommend you to a higher post in the organization.

Certain salient factors emerge from this thinking, each of which should play an important role in the lifestyle of anyone who expects to be a successful middle manager.

Strive to Be an Achiever

Your goal to achieve long-term success should help you to motivate your employees and manage your boss. Where to start? First, give yourself a new name. Say to yourself, "I am an achiever." Start reading books on management. There is a good reason why *The Search for Excellence, The One-Minute Manager, The Passion for Excellence,* and *Iacocca* remain on the best-seller lists for many months. People aren't reading them for fun. They are reading them to learn, so that they can become more knowledgeable in the world of business.

How do you become an achiever? You must have a plan, a direction, one that keeps your responsibilities to both your boss and to your subordinates in perspective and in balance.

ROGERS' RULES FOR BECOMING AN ACHIEVER

1. Decide what results you hope to achieve.

2. Set a time frame for yourself.

3. Convey this information clearly to your subordinates and to your boss.

4. Demand a high performance from yourself and convey to your team that you expect an equally high performance from them.

5. When things go wrong (as they inevitably will), refrain from

being shattered. Get yourself and your team quickly back on the right track.

6. Keep the pressure to excel on both yourself and your subordinates, but make it *positive pressure*. Gung-ho enthusiasm and confidence in your abilities and those of your team is positive pressure that motivates people to want to do more and to do better. *Negative pressure*, typified by stress and the fear of making a mistake, has exactly the opposite effect.

7. Monitor your own performance as well as theirs on a continuing basis, so that any fall-off can be spotted and corrected in good time.

Communicating Your Way Toward Your Goal of Motivating and Managing

I have dealt with this subject before, but I am back to it again because every achiever must be a communicator, and communication is number one on the list of business problems. Remember that as a middle manager, you must communicate both up and down the executive ladder with equal facility and clarity. Your boss must know what you are doing, and your subordinates must know what you expect of them. It sounds simple, but it isn't.

In my years in public relations, I've seen a careerful of misunderstandings, mine as well as those of other people. In retrospect, I've been able to pinpoint the causes; the culprit is almost invariably one of the "big six" barriers to communication.

ROGERS' BARRIERS TO COMMUNICATION

1. We don't always mean exactly what we say. Most of us contend otherwise, but I'm sure you remember many instances

when you have replied to your business associates, your spouse, or your friend, "Well, maybe I did say that, but that's not what I meant to say." Unfortunately, very few of us are able to articulate in our speech what we are saying to ourselves in our heads.

2. Mixed signals: Our "body language" says one thing while our mouth is saying another. We tell someone that we're calm and peaceful while we are pacing up and down the room biting our fingernails.

3. We listen between the lines and hear what we want to hear. I have mentioned before that most of us have a listening problem. Our minds wander. We are thinking of what we want to say in response, and we consequently select, out of the torrent of words that are thrown at us in any conversation, the few phrases that we have preconditioned ourselves to hear.

4. Our acceptance or rejection of what someone says is largely dependent on whether we like him or dislike him. It's difficult to buck human nature. That's how life is. The natural tendency is to accept as gospel almost anything that is said by the man or woman you love, and you will most likely reject the most sane, logical argument from your mother-in-law who offended you many years ago. Apply this principle in varying degrees to the business world, and you will note how easily it becomes a difficult barrier to communication.

5. Words mean different things to different people. Most professions not only have their own technical jargon, they also have specific "technical" meanings for words in common use outside the profession. As I wrote in an earlier chapter, I always ask lawyers and accountants to translate into lay English whatever they have said—or written.

6. The worst offender: we just aren't paying attention. This happens to all of us. I remind you once more to think of the many times you have said to someone in the midst of a conversa-

tion, "What did you just say?" He hadn't dropped his voice. You heard him, but at that moment you weren't paying attention to what he was saying.

Don't give up. You will never be able to eliminate communication foul-ups entirely. But if you think about the big six barriers to communication, if you remind yourself about them constantly, you will have done a great deal to lick the problem.

I have spent much time in this book on communication. I have already given you Rogers' Rules for Communication, but I feel that the subject is sufficiently important for me to repeat myself. I suspect that you may have already forgotten my first set of rules on this subject. If you have, read on. If they impressed you so much that they are now indelibly etched into your brain, you have my unequivocal approval to skip them and move on to the next section.

ROGERS' RULES FOR COMMUNICATION

1. Put yourself in the other person's shoes. Look at what you are saying from his point of view.

2. Try to get a reaction after you have made a statement. Did he really understand what you were trying to say?

3. Written or oral communication alone can give an incorrect impression. Use the "one-two punch." Follow up a written letter or memo with a one-on-one conversation reiterating the major points. Follow up a verbal understanding with a confirmation letter or memo.

4. In speaking, organize your thoughts in a logical progression. Don't jump around; have an outline in mind so that the discussion flows from one point to the next until reaching the conclusion.

5. Use simple language. The simpler your statement, the better chance you have of communicating effectively.

6. While speaking or listening, look the other person in the eye. To get through to someone, you must first make contact.

A Fish Stinks from the Head

Achieving results is what management is all about. There are three kinds of managers:

- Those who make things happen;
- Those who watch things happen around them and watch the parade go by;
- Those who have no idea what is happening.

Your job is to get into the first category and stay there.

The manager who blames his staff for anything that goes wrong in his department is making a mistake. His success will be limited unless and until he learns that he is responsible for everything that goes on in his department, both good and bad. If he is going to take credit for all the accomplishments that occur, he must also be willing to take the blame for the gaffes, the errors, and the crises.

There is an ancient saying that applies here. Some say it comes from Eastern European Jewish folklore, others that it stems from the Greeks. I first heard it many years ago from my father, who told me, "A fish stinks from the head." If this image is too graphic for you, it may be more palatable to translate it into Harry Truman's phrase, "The buck stops here." In your department, you're the buck stopper.

Developing Your Subordinates

I say it all the time, and I'm not alone—thousands of other executives in service businesses say it, too. "My only assets go up and down the elevator every day." The people who work for me are my primary investment in our business. They cost money to acquire and maintain (did you ever compute the twenty-two percent in fringe benefits that it costs for every employee in your company?), and their value increases as they become more effective in their jobs and capable of taking on greater responsibility.

People learn by doing. Experience is still the greatest teacher, and we encourage our managers to spend time planning the experience of anyone who appears to have potential for development. This means developing people gradually, step by step, not dumping increased duties upon them before they are ready.

As a middle manager, it is your responsibility to train your subordinates so that they can step into your job when you move up. Your people will learn how to manage if you give them the opportunity to manage under your guidance. Don't be afraid that you're going to "develop" yourself out of a job by training your subordinates to take over. All the upper-level executives I know believe that the ability to "bring people along" is one of the most desirable qualities a manager can have. You will be doing your own career a favor if you can develop your people by discussing problems with them, taking them into your confidence, and involving them in decisions you must make.

ROGERS' RULES FOR DEVELOPING SUBORDINATES

1. Let them know you are grooming them for bigger and better things.

2. Give subordinates the opportunity to manage under your guidance. Explain to them how to tackle a job senior to the one for which they are presently responsible.

3. Discuss with them the outcome of their performance.

4. Use mistakes as teaching opportunities, even for those not directly involved. Make it "safe" to make mistakes—this is how learning happens!

5. Don't be selfish with your knowledge. You won't keep a talented subordinate from leapfrogging over you by denying him your advice and counseling.

Let a Smile Be Your Umbrella

Successful middle managers learn to laugh at their own actions and attitudes. You will find that it is much easier to get along with both bosses and subordinates if you have a sense of humor about yourself. Although many bosses tend to be pompous and full of themselves, this stuffed-shirt posture generates resentment, even contempt, from those who have to deal with it. A boss with a sense of humor about himself commands respect and admiration; the capacity to laugh at your own foibles is one of the things that makes you human. As R. Paul Toeppen, a business executive friend of mine, puts it, "Do I have a sense of humor with my employees? I hope so. I regard it as extremely important. Not a condition of continuous joking or practical jokes; rather, a light, easy, relaxed manner and atmosphere. I find little constructive effort in a tense, guarded atmosphere."

When the office is tense or depressed, a sense of humor often helps to defuse explosive situations or restore a healthy attitude and put everyone back on a productive, even keel.

I asked J. Fred Bucy, former president of Texas Instruments, to give me his observations on the importance of humor in the business world. Mr. Bucy wrote, "I feel that having a sense of humor is almost essential. You can get by without one, but your life's work goes a lot easier if the boss has a sense of humor. Many times the appropriate humor can prevent a very tense situation from becoming even more serious. Having a sense of humor humanizes the boss faster than anyone else. . . . In my practice of management I have tried to use humor whenever it has seemed appropriate, especially to relax people in the face of a particularly serious problem. Humor helps people get acquainted with one another and can be very helpful in this instance."

I get a laugh from my employees when I recount for them my misadventures in the land of the VCR. Millions of people throughout the world are using them, so I probably remain one of the few people in existence who must still pore through the instruction booklet before I can get that picture to finally appear on the screen.

My associates also like to hear me reminisce about my clumsiness in the earlier days, particularly stories that involve my son, who is now the president of our company. I tell them about getting a flat tire while driving up the Rhine River in Germany. I had no idea how to even start to change a tire and watched with great discomfort and annoyance as ten-year-old Ron, already aware of his father's inadequacies in these areas, took over and changed the tire in ten minutes.

They laugh when I recall to them that in my attempts to be a loving father, I took Ron to ball games when the Dodgers first came to Los Angeles. It wasn't until we suffered through four games together that we discovered that we both hated baseball (a heretical statement to make in the Los Angeles community). He went to indulge his old man. I went because I was told that every red-blooded American boy loved baseball. We both decided that there were better things that we could do with our time.

Don't take the Don Rickles/Joan Rivers approach and make fun of others. Having a sense of humor is not the same thing as being the office put-down comic. From time to time every office seems to acquire someone who makes jokes at others' expense. This is not fun or even funny; it is nothing short of bullying. No one appreciates being the butt of these kinds of jokes, but all too often the targets are the easy marks, the most fragile egos in the office. If this seems to be the habit of one of your employees, put a stop to it before it affects office morale.

ROGERS' RULES FOR OFFICE HUMOR

1. Lighten up. Poke fun at yourself and enjoy it. After all, some of the things you do really are funny.

2. Don't tolerate making fun of others, either in yourself or in those who report to you.

3. Use humor as a "safety valve," with yourself as the target. When you see an associate having a hard time, tell an anecdote about when you had a similar (or worse) disaster.

4. The best source of humor is the daily goings-on in the office. The things that happen to all of us—from being put on "hold" to the perennially malfunctioning copy machine—are the equalizers that forge a bond of humor between employer and employee.

5. Avoid "insider" humor in front of nonemployees. You make your associates feel uncomfortable about your sharing office experiences with outsiders.

6. Share with your co-workers the things that make you laugh. Comic strips and anecdotes make the rounds in our office. Cartoons sent from one branch of our offices to another increase the sense of camaraderie among our staff.

Tact and Diplomacy

Tact and diplomacy are not merely two skills you ought to have. They also ought to be skills that you impart to your subordinates. Saying the wrong thing at the wrong time, or even the right thing the wrong way—is a fear of many young professionals. You want to prevent what used to be called "the tongue and toenail sandwich." The removal of your foot from your mouth once you've put it there is an art, and one that definitely improves with practice.

In the public relations business, tact and diplomacy must become second nature, so I hope you'll forgive me for telling a self-serving anecdote. It's a story that the writer, William L. Simon, here says that I'd forgotten. Nevertheless, it illustrates very well the arts of tact and diplomacy.

Dear Mr. Rogers:

I'd like to share with you my favorite Henry Rogers story. It happened so fleetingly that I wonder if you consciously recorded the event.

Several years ago I was hired by Universal to write a theatrical short promoting the DeLorean motorcar, and was sent over to have a meeting with you.

While we were talking in your office, a question came up about the handling of the film. You stepped across to Warren Cowan's office to consult with him and, with the doors open, I could hear what took place.

In Mr. Cowan's office, you encountered Zsa Zsa Gabor. After the initial exchange of greetings, you said, "Zsa Zsa, I've always wanted to tell you, I've been a fan of yours all my life." I could imagine the look on Zsa Zsa's face. You immediately amended: "All your life."

*Your remarks showed one of the talents that undoubtedly has
accounted for your success in dealing with people. As soon as
you had spoken, you recognized your words as something that a
lady—especially a lady like Zsa Zsa—would not appreciate.
Though the project we were discussing never got made, I've
remembered that moment ever since. I wanted to share it with
you because if you've forgotten the incident, recalling it now
may amuse you.*

Sincerely,

*William L. Simon, Ph.D.
Rancho Santa Fe, California*

One night at the Pierre Hotel in New York, I sat at an elegant
black-tie dinner party, tense and nervous, hoping and praying
that the guest speaker would be tactful and diplomatic. Our
company was responsible for this event, which was hosted by Sir
Adam Thompson, chairman of British Caledonian Airways, our
client. The client had just launched British Caledonian's first
daily London-to-New York service, and Sir Adam had arrived
that afternoon on the inaugural flight with a planeload of his
personal guests—British titled gentlemen, lords of the manor, so
to speak, as well as distinguished bankers and business executives. It had been our responsibility to supplement his guest list
with a number of equally distinguished New Yorkers, which we
had done. We had also been asked to recruit a guest speaker for
the evening, using our own discretion to select someone who
would be appropriate for the occasion, and to pay him or her an
honorarium that would make economic sense to the client. This
was a tall order, but we had performed similar services for clients
a hundred times before and we were up to it.

We had only been given three weeks advance notice to get a

speaker. Who did we want? Was he or she available? Who would the guests be most interested in? A politician, an actor, a comedian, an economist, a government official? Lecture agents have hundreds of speakers on their client lists. We began to think of likely names. Ex-presidents are available for substantial fees— Richard Nixon, Gerald Ford, Jimmy Carter? We ruled them out. Johnny Carson, Milton Berle, Shirley MacLaine, Ann Landers, Mayor Koch, Walter Cronkite, Dan Rather, Milton Friedman, William Safire, and fifty other names were all suggested. For one reason or another we rejected them. Then suddenly someone said "Barbara Walters," and we all responded—favorably and enthusiastically. Could we get her? We had no idea. We decided to try. One of my associates knew her very well and offered to telephone her. Five minutes later she came back, smiling but a bit apprehensive.

"Barbara will do it," she said, "but under certain conditions. She has another party to go to that night so she will have to leave by nine-thirty. She will arrive at seven-thirty for cocktails, dinner at eight, she'll speak from nine until nine-thirty, and then she'll be gone."

"Did you ask her the price?" I asked.

"Her fee is $____!"

I gulped. The amount was well into five figures, and that was for a two-hour appearance and a thirty-minute talk. Television commentators do very well, I thought.

One more question. "Did you ask her what she would talk about?"

"I told her who the audience would be. She told me she would think of something appropriate and we would have to leave the subject matter to her discretion."

We looked at each other. I finally nodded and said, "Let's go. Let's take a chance." Everyone agreed, and three minutes later we had a confirmation from Barbara Walters.

For three weeks I worried about the decision. Why? It was more than having the client pleased or displeased about our decision. It was more than spending a sizable sum of the client's money. No, it was because I felt a strong sense of responsibility to the chairman. He was hosting a large group of friends and acquaintances who had made a five-thousand-mile trip at his invitation. If they were bored or simply disinterested in what Barbara Walters had to say, they wouldn't blame Rogers & Cowan or Henry Rogers. They had no idea who we were. They would blame their host, Sir Adam Thompson. That is why I was worried. I was totally responsible, and even after my many years of business experience, I have as strong a feeling of responsibility today towards our clients as I did twenty-five years ago.

The evening arrived. Barbara Walters made her entrance at precisely seven-thirty and mingled with the guests during the cocktail reception. She was seated next to Sir Adam at dinner. At nine o'clock, she was introduced and stepped to the rostrum. She was welcomed with mild applause; I got the impression that most of the audience did not know that Barbara Walters was one of America's most distinguished television commentators. I began to fidget. What was she going to talk about? Would they be bored? Would some of the guests suddenly get up and head for the men's room?

Barbara smiled at her audience, and I'll paraphrase her opening remark: "I decided to talk with you this evening on three subjects who I recently interviewed on the ABC Television Network—your prime minister, Margaret Thatcher; your Prince of Wales, Charles; and of course, your favorite singer of all time, Boy George!"

The moment she mentioned Margaret Thatcher everyone sat up in their chairs with smiles on their faces; at the mention of Prince Charles they began to giggle; and when she mentioned

Boy George, an incongruous contrast to the first two, they were laughing out loud—and they didn't stop laughing for half an hour. Barbara told one amusing anecdote after another about three people to whom her audience related. They loved her and they loved the half hour of entertainment she provided. Hers was a remarkable performance. She poked fun, and her audience ate it up, just as an American audience would have laughed if she had poked fun at President Reagan, Nancy Reagan, Michael Jackson, and Madonna. At nine-thirty she stepped away from the rostrum to a standing ovation, said goodnight to her host and the others at her table, and quietly left the room through a back door with the applause resounding in her ears.

This was the best example of the use of tact and diplomacy that I had seen in many, many years. The ability to size up your audience, to decide what will appeal to them, to say the right thing at the right time, and to walk out of the spotlight with people still applauding your efforts, is a rare talent to which we should all aspire.

The evening was a triumph for British Caledonian Airways. I was of course gratified when Sir Adam expressed his thanks to me for the contribution that Rogers & Cowan had made to the event. That made all the worrying worthwhile.

ROGERS' RULES FOR TACT AND DIPLOMACY

1. Tact and diplomacy are grounded in politeness. If you weren't brought up on Emily Post, that's no excuse.

2. Learn to say the right thing at the right time.

3. Do not tolerate rudeness in your subordinates, either to you or to others. Tell the offender in the privacy of his or your office that such behavior is unacceptable.

4. Learn and teach the benefits of silence. When you don't know what to say, often the best course of action is not to say anything.

Consistent, Reliable, Dependable

The people I value most at Rogers & Cowan are those who are consistent and reliable. The steady players, the "Rocks of Gibraltar," are the key people at any level of an organization because they have the ability to tackle any crisis that comes along. That knowledge, that confidence, helps the boss—me—to sleep at night. When the roof begins to fall in, I may not know *what* my steady players are going to do, but I do know *how* they are going to do it—rationally, systematically, and thoroughly. "He's dependable" is a reputation built over time, but once established, it becomes one of the finest compliments anyone can pay you in the business world.

What's the key? It's the same at any level of management, from the top to the bottom: *no surprises.*

Each time you surprise your boss or your subordinates by your actions, you are devaluing yourself in their eyes. Although the best choice is not to blow up when things go wrong, it's still far better for your secretary to be able to say "I bet he's going to have a fit when he sees this"—and be right—than to be taken aback because you fly off the handle when she least expects it.

ROGERS' RULES FOR RELIABILITY

1. Be predictable. Say what you are going to do. Do what you say you're going to do.

2. Seek out responsibility. Pitch in without being asked. Confront problems squarely.

3. Don't make promises you can't keep. The business world is full of people who are afraid of disappointing others by saying no. Instead, they say yes when they don't mean it, which in the long run is far more disappointing.

The "Carnation" Technique

One person who excels at motivating and managing people is Dodger manager Tommy Lasorda. According to Tommy, he got the idea from his mother, who showed him the slogan on a can of Carnation milk that read, "Contented cows give better milk."

"I learned something from that," he said. "I feel contented ballplayers give better performances. I want to treat ballplayers the way I wanted to be treated when I played. The guys I really enjoyed playing for are the guys who made me feel I was really an important part of the team. I try to make my players feel very important. Make them feel wanted, appreciated. I try to get them to be proud of the uniform they're wearing and be proud of themselves." With an attitude like that, I'd go to bat for Tommy myself.

Running a Marathon

Why does a person who is not terribly interested in his work at the office stretch himself to the limit running a marathon? What makes him run? The answer is that he is trying to beat himself, beat a stopwatch, or beat other people. The long-distance runner has set himself a goal, and because he has a goal he will force himself to run farther or faster than he ever thought he could.

If you can carry this attitude from competitive sports into the office, you can motivate your subordinates to reach even the most optimistic objectives. The best way to get that spirit of

competitive sports into the workplace is to establish some goals—
to give your subordinates an opportunity to go up against something or somebody. What you are providing is a way to keep
score.

Comparing your work to sports may also teach both you and
your subordinates how to cope with failure. One of the big
impediments to a fully committed, highly motivated state of
mind is preoccupation with failure. If you point out to your
people that there are wins and losses for everyone in any
competitive sport, they will begin to look at their jobs in a
different light. John McEnroe, Muhammed Ali, Dorothy
Hamill—nobody gets to the top of the field by being afraid to
lose.

In the public relations business, there are certain media outlets
that are a challenge, and our people compete amongst themselves to convince key outlets to cover the clients for whom they
are responsible. They all know what the goals are. No one has to
tell them. A feature in *The New York Times*, *Washington Post*,
Los Angeles Times, and *Wall Street Journal* is high on the priority
list for accounts. Appearances on "Today," "Good Morning
America," and "CBS Morning News" are worthy of a gold star.
For our show-business clients, page-one coverage in *Daily Variety* and *Hollywood Reporter* is important. In our motion picture
division, articles in *Time* and *Newsweek* or a photo layout in *Life*
are all high on the "We Must Get" list. For television, it's a *TV
Guide* cover, and features in *Fortune*, *Business Week*, and *Forbes*
are always sought for our corporate clients.

It is healthy that our publicists think of these media objectives
as they do a competitive sport. Some of them have magazine
covers for which they have been responsible framed and hung on
their walls just as athletes decorate their rooms with trophies they
have won.

Get your subordinates to feel that they are playing a game and you will find yourself the leader of an ambitious, aggressive, motivated team.

Massaging the Boss's Ego

We all have egos. Most of us have egos that don't get in our way or adversely affect the people with whom we work. Everybody's ego needs a little bolstering now and then. Some people, however, have enlarged egos that require constant stroking and massaging. If your boss falls into this category, then your logical approach is to brush up on your stroking and massaging skills.

This may sound offensive to you. Is Henry recommending toadyism and apple polishing? Hardly. I am recommending that you take a course in people relations. You do certain things to accommodate your spouse and your children. You make a point of getting along with friends and acquaintances. I've spent most of this book advising you on how to get along with your subordinates and how to motivate them to give their best possible performance. I have told you that each of your subordinates needs personal attention, one-on-one handling. You can't treat each of them the same way, for they are individuals, and you have to figure out how to get the best results out of each of them. Your boss is one more person in your life who you must deal with. He's one of the most important people in your life, and he deserves at least as much of your personal attention as anyone else. Each person you deal with in business is a problem, each one is a challenge. Instead of shrinking away from the fact that your boss has an enlarged ego, consider it a challenge and figure out a way to handle it—and him—without demeaning yourself.

The Rogers Massage Method doesn't have to be painful, and I certainly don't believe that it involves any groveling on your part.

I endorse it not only because it works but because I believe that you may actually come to enjoy it. Incredible? Impossible? Insanity? There is a method to my madness. Read on.

I've said it before. I'll say it again. Make it into a game. You and your boss are players in the game, but you have an enormous advantage, because you're the only one who knows it's being played.

Figure out subtle massage treatments that make him feel good about himself and his abilities. He'll feel good about you for having done so. If he wants you to bring him a shiny apple every morning (I'm being facetious), then bring him a shiny apple every morning. A memo from you to him: "I just read that report you sent to management yesterday. Brilliant!" Not a long paean of praise. That's too obvious. Short and to the point. Here are some other examples. Select those which you feel are applicable to your boss's personality:

> "That's a handsome tie you're wearing today."
> "Are you on a diet? You look much thinner."
> "Did you see that girl give you the eye?"
> "Would you give me some advice please on this problem?"
> "It's a cinch for you but I just can't seem to figure it out."
> "You handled the staff meeting exceptionally well today."
> "You always seem to come up with the right answers. I wish I could do that."
> "I loved the way you told that guy off. He deserved it."

Don't let this approach trouble you. You're not doing anyone any harm. On the contrary, you're making someone else feel good (even though he may not deserve it at the moment) and—most important of all—you will probably be furthering your own career. Your boss, despite or maybe because of his ego problems, may move up to be president one day, and he will want someone working closely with him who truly understands him.

What is the price you pay if you ignore the boss's need to be massaged? Let me tell you of one of my own experiences. Although I don't have a boss because I have always run my own business, I really have a hundred bosses. Every client is a boss, and just as you must figure out how to manage your boss, I always have to figure out how to manage each client. There are times when I fail.

I received a phone call from David Foster's secretary; Mr. Foster had recently been named president of Colgate-Palmolive. She indicated that he would like to meet with me at my earliest convenience. I had developed a very warm relationship with David Foster while he was head of the Household Products Division of the company. We had handled a number of product assignments for him and he had been most complimentary about our work.

I met with him shortly thereafter in his elegant walnut-paneled office overlooking Park Avenue. After a warm exchange of greetings, he explained that he had just decided that Colgate-Palmolive would become heavily involved in women's sports events, and that the company would use this new approach to promote its products. He had already locked up the first event and wanted Rogers & Cowan to handle public relations for it. It was the Colgate-Dinah Shore Women's Circle Golf Tournament.

"Lay out a plan," he said. "We must get started immediately, and," he added, "once you get this under way we'll talk about other events we are scheduling for this program."

With hundreds of thousands of dollars dancing in my head, I returned to my office to confer with my associates about the development of a public relations program for the upcoming tournament. A few days later I was back in David Foster's office with plan in hand. A half hour later I left with his full approval of the plan and an agreement on fee and expenses for the project.

Our first step was to announce Colgate's sponsorship for a women's sports program at a press conference at the Plaza Hotel in New York. I telephoned Dinah Shore, a longtime friend, confirmed the date with her, and then the Rogers & Cowan troops went into action. The guest list included not only the media—press, television, and radio—but a number of women sports figures and of course, Mr. Foster and his staff.

At 10 A.M. the meeting room was jammed. The media were interested in Colgate's new involvement in women's sports and were intrigued with the participation of Dinah Shore, who at that time was one of television's leading personalities. At 10:05, Mr. Foster stepped up to the rostrum, and to the accompaniment of much flashbulb popping and other media fanfare, read the prepared announcement. Then he introduced Dinah Shore. She said how pleased she was to participate in this precedent-shattering program (it was the first of its kind), and she then proceeded to introduce the women professional golfers and sports figures who were also there. More flashbulbs.

Although the official press conference was over, the media had not yet had its fill. Each reporter wanted his own exclusive interview with Dinah Shore. Sports writers clustered around tennis great Althea Gibson and the other women sports celebrities. My associates and I were kept very busy helping each member of the media get what they needed to complete their coverage. A half hour later the room cleared out. Mr. Foster and his associates congratulated us for a job well done, and we all went back to our offices.

In the short run we were a big success. Each local and network TV station carried the news that night and the following morning; all the New York papers gave it big text and photo coverage; the Associated Press and United Press International filed stories. We had every reason to be pleased with ourselves.

You can imagine my surprise when a letter arrived a few days later from Colgate-Palmolive. We had been discharged. After careful consideration, the company had decided that Rogers & Cowan was not right for this assignment and had made other plans for public relations representation. To add insult to injury, the letter was written not by David Foster but by a Colgate middle management executive.

I tried to get in touch with David Foster. I put in a call. He was out. I tried eight times in the next three days. It became apparent that he didn't want to talk to me. I called the young man who had written the letter. He took my call but couldn't really tell me anything. He was just acting on orders. Saddened, disappointed, confused, I went on to other matters and other clients. I didn't even have the benefit of learning from the experience because I couldn't find out what had gone wrong.

Five years went by. One day I read in *The New York Times* that the public relations head of Colgate-Palmolive was about to retire. I was in New York a few days later and invited him to a farewell lunch. We spent a pleasant hour together, until I finally asked him the question that had gone unanswered for so long. "Now that you've retired," I said, "would you please tell me why David Foster fired us after that Dinah Shore press conference five years ago?"

He looked at me in wonderment. "I can't believe you!" he exclaimed. "Are you telling me you have no idea why you were discharged?"

"Honestly," I replied. "I tried my best to find out at the time, but to this day I have no idea."

"For a guy who's been around as long as you have, I'm surprised you couldn't figure it out for yourself. David fired you for ego reasons," he explained. "Dinah got all the play. She was on television. He wasn't. Her picture was in the papers. His wasn't."

"But I can't control the media," I responded.

"Of course not. And he understands that. Where you blew it was after the press conference. You were helping the media get to Dinah, not to him. Of course they wanted to talk to Dinah, but with your know-how you could have steered some of them his way. Even if they hadn't used any of his quotes, he would have known that you'd given it your best shot. David's a good executive and he's fair, but he needed his ego massaged. If you had pushed the media in his direction you'd probably still be working for Colgate."

I sat there stunned at my own shortsightedness. Despite the fact that I had warned my associates about this countless times, I had made the unpardonable mistake of forgetting who my client was. My client was not Dinah Shore. My client was not even Colgate-Palmolive. Companies are abstractions. Clients are people. My client was David Foster. The client has the power to hire you or fire you. He is the one who orders the check to be signed or not signed.

Who can hire and fire you? Who signs your checks? Your first, best, and most important client is your boss. In your business life it will be to your advantage to remember this. It will also be to your advantage to massage his ego if that is what he needs. It's one way to manage your boss.

Managing Your Boss

Do you think that it's easier to manage your subordinates than to manage your boss? Do you believe that you are unable to influence the way he behaves toward you? Let's return to our game theory and the need to break the cycle with a boss who is often unpleasant to deal with. You begin to massage his ego in the hope that he will be more accommodating toward you. Let's talk about why you would want to do that. You have certain needs, certain wants, certain career aspirations. He is in a position to help you get them. What about him? He also has certain needs, certain wants, certain career aspirations. It follows that you can get what you want by helping him get what he wants.

This is where the Golden Rule comes in: Do unto others as you would have them do unto you. Once more I suggest that you put yourself in the other person's shoes. If you are cool and standoffish, expect to be treated the same way. If you regard your boss as a dictator, expect to be treated like a serf. If you act with strength, responsibility, and loyalty, he will come to manage you in the same way. You must be prepared, however, to make the first move and also to give the relationship time to develop.

Once you realize that you can manage your boss, you must develop a plan to achieve your objective. Let me stress that "manage" is a positive verb, not a negative one. We're not dealing with manipulation or influence with ulterior motives in mind. Your objective is forthright and aboveboard. Your objective is to help both you and your boss do a better job.

Evaluate him, both as a human being and as a boss. Then evaluate yourself. What kind of person is he? What kind of person are you? In what areas are you in agreement? How do you differ? You would be horrified at the thought that he would try to change you, so don't get the wayward notion that you are going to change him. Accept both of you for what you are, then develop your relationship from there. Build on your individual and joint strengths and learn to accommodate the weakness that you are both burdened with.

Your next step is to figure out where your boss needs help. Everyone needs, wants, and appreciates help. Even your boss. Take a look at his work habits and you will soon spot where you can be of greatest service to him. If he's a poor writer, offer to help him draft interoffice memos or correspondence. If he's a "sandwich-at-the-desk" person, make lunch productive by offering to join him a few times a week with your own brown paper bag. If he seems disorganized, offer to work up agendas and outlines for meetings and presentations. You will find a hundred ways to help him if you become perceptive and look for ways to make him look good. By doing so, you are changing the way he thinks about you and enhancing your own career.

By doing this, are you "changing" him? I said earlier that you cannot change people. I didn't say that you cannot influence their behavior, making it easier for them to change themselves. You *can* influence your boss's behavior for the good by directing and guiding him in ways that will improve his own performance and make your own life more pleasant and more productive.

What about rewards? Can you reward your boss? You bet. I'm sure you are skeptical. I assure you that it works at least as well as rewarding your subordinates.

ROGERS' RULES FOR REWARDING YOUR BOSS

1. He must be doing something right. Praise him for it.
2. Tell others about his accomplishments. It will get back to him.
3. Feed him recommendations about how he can improve the performance of his department.
4. Volunteer to help him train the new employees he brings on board.
5. Let him know that you are proud to work for him and for the company.

Your career depends on how you handle, how you treat, how you motivate, how you massage, how you manage the people you work with. In your middle management position, you must manage down and manage up as well. It is the essence of managerial premises that you treat those above and below you equally—with respect, courtesy, and kindness, while constantly helping them to improve their performance. You will find that if you handle your superiors and subordinates in this way, you will have little trouble moving from middle management to top management.

Conclusion

The time has come to sit back and think about what you just read. You spent your hard-earned money to buy the book. Was it worth it? Did you get anything out of it? Can you be a better manager tomorrow than you are today because of it? The answer to that is for you to determine. If you put it back on your bookshelf and don't even try to put into practice any of the "rules" or the advice that I have offered you in this book, then you have wasted your money and your time. I am afraid that could happen. I believe it normally happens, because if everyone practiced what is preached in the many hundreds of books that are written every year on success, management, fitness, health, diet, and love, we would be a nation of loving, fit, healthy, successful people. Unfortunately a good percentage of the people who have read these books are still as fat, unfit, unsuccessful, and unloving as they always were.

What to do about it? I don't want you to feel that you have wasted your time and money. I don't expect that you will try to memorize the contents of this book or that you will reread it so that some of the rules will sink in. No, instead I'm going to make it easy for you. I'll summarize the entire book in just a few pages. Then I'll ask you to pick up and reread these pages once a week for the next three or four months. If you do that, I can guarantee that at the end of that time you will be a better manager than you are today. Fair enough? Let's go.

ROGERS' RULES FOR MIDDLE MANAGERS WHO HAVE SOLVED THE TWO-HAT PROBLEM WITH THE ONE-HAT SOLUTION

1. I will live by the principle of the Golden Rule. I am going to treat people as I would like them to treat me.

2. I will delegate authority to my associates, but I'll do it in easy stages. I won't dump everything on them at once.

3. My subordinates and I will come to an agreement on their priorities, and my boss and I will come to a similar agreement.

4. I will give my employees feedback and coaching, thereby improving their performance, and I will encourage my boss to do the same for me.

5. I will not evaluate members of my team by their past performance—good or bad—but rather, by their present performance.

6. I'll give my subordinates credit when I believe it is due them, remembering that it is better to give than not to give.

7. I'll try to make my employees feel important, because I know that with self-respect and self-esteem comes added motivation.

8. I will try not to impose my will on my employees, but

instead will seek mutual decisions that will determine their eventual course of action.

9. I'll serve as a role model to my subordinates, even though at times I'll think about Pagliacci singing, "Even though your heart is breaking, laugh clown, laugh."

10. I'll build a winning team by giving my employees one-on-one attention, with emphasis on the importance of working together as a team.

11. I'll lose an occasional skirmish with those who report to me because I know that over the long pull it will help me to emerge a winner. This is my "lose-the-battle-and-win-the-war" theory.

12. I shall try my best to prevent the Peter Principle from taking a major hold in my department by not elevating my employees to their level of incompetence.

13. Once I have built a team I am proud of, I'll fight hard for my people, trying to get for them all the perks that are available to everyone else in the organization.

14. I shall listen to my employees—and to my boss. Not only listen, but *comprehend*.

15. I shall take notes, and encourage my people to do the same.

16. I'll speak plainly and clearly and make certain that my subordinates and boss understand what I mean to say as well as what I actually say.

17. I'll ask questions of employees and my boss, because I understand that asking questions is the only way for me to know what is going on around me.

18. I'll dish out constructive criticism when necessary, but will always sandwich it between two layers of praise.

19. I'll accept criticism graciously and without rancor, whether it is justified or not. People will know that I can dish it out, but that I can take it too.

20. I'll find reasons to praise my associates, because praise increases the level of performance. I'll also praise my boss at proper times because it will enhance my relationship with him.

21. I'll say no to my subordinates in such a tactful manner that they will not resent my rejection.

22. I'll do the same with my boss, remembering that tact and diplomacy will prevent him from being turned off by me.

23. I'll be ready to say "I don't know" to my boss, and I will encourage my subordinates to say "I don't know" to me.

24. I'll admit when I am wrong, and I will encourage my people to recognize that saying "I am wrong" is a sign of strength, not weakness.

25. I'll organize my work day so that I will always have time to meet with my staff, collectively and individually.

26. I'll encourage my boss to spend time with me.

27. I will set up a list of guidelines for hiring people.

28. I'll have the guts to fire someone when necessary, but I will do it as painlessly for him as possible.

29. If I get fired, I'll accept it tactfully, making certain not to offend my boss or associates who I leave behind.

30. I'll get outside advice before making a final decision to quit my job.

31. When I decide to quit, I will know that it's a gamble that my boss could discover my intention and fire me before I get another job.

32. I'll make a game out of handling my difficult boss, and I will retain a sense of humor about my relationship with him.

33. I'll cope as best I can with Complainers, Basket Cases, Clams and Ix-nayers.

34. I accept that "a fish stinks from the head" and that the quality of work turned out by my team is my responsibility. If it's lousy, I'm to blame. If it's good, I'll take the credit.

35. A sense of humor about my job and its problems is essential, and if things get tough I'll sing, "Let a Smile Be Your Umbrella."

36. I realize that money isn't everything, and that my people must be rewarded with special perks for special performance.

37. I know that I must manage my boss and motivate my employees. That is the road to my future success.